RED ARMY RESURGENT

Other Publications:
THE EPIC OF FLIGHT
THE GOOD COOK
THE SEAFARERS
THE ENCYCLOPEDIA OF COLLECTIBLES
THE GREAT CITIES
HOME REPAIR AND IMPROVEMENT
THE WORLD'S WILD PLACES
THE TIME-LIFE LIBRARY OF BOATING
HUMAN BEHAVIOR
THE ART OF SEWING
THE OLD WEST
THE EMERGENCE OF MAN
THE AMERICAN WILDERNESS
THE TIME-LIFE ENCYCLOPEDIA OF GARDENING
LIFE LIBRARY OF PHOTOGRAPHY
THIS FABULOUS CENTURY
FOODS OF THE WORLD
TIME-LIFE LIBRARY OF AMERICA
TIME-LIFE LIBRARY OF ART
GREAT AGES OF MAN
LIFE SCIENCE LIBRARY
THE LIFE HISTORY OF THE UNITED STATES
TIME READING PROGRAM
LIFE NATURE LIBRARY
LIFE WORLD LIBRARY
FAMILY LIBRARY:
  HOW THINGS WORK IN YOUR HOME
  THE TIME-LIFE BOOK OF THE FAMILY CAR
  THE TIME-LIFE FAMILY LEGAL GUIDE
  THE TIME-LIFE BOOK OF FAMILY FINANCE

Previous World War II Volumes:
Prelude to War
Blitzkrieg
The Battle of Britain
The Rising Sun
The Battle of the Atlantic
Russia Besieged
The War in the Desert
The Home Front: U.S.A.
China-Burma-India
Island Fighting
The Italian Campaign
Partisans and Guerrillas
The Second Front
Liberation
Return to the Philippines
The Air War in Europe
The Resistance
The Battle of the Bulge
The Road to Tokyo

WORLD WAR II · TIME-LIFE BOOKS · ALEXANDRIA, VIRGINIA

BY JOHN SHAW
AND THE EDITORS OF TIME-LIFE BOOKS

RED ARMY RESURGENT

Time-Life Books Inc.
is a wholly owned subsidiary of
TIME INCORPORATED

Founder: Henry R. Luce 1898-1967

Editor-in-Chief: Henry Anatole Grunwald
Chairman of the Board: Andrew Heiskell
President: James R. Shepley
Editorial Director: Ralph Graves
Vice Chairman: Arthur Temple

TIME-LIFE BOOKS INC.

Managing Editor: Jerry Korn
Executive Editor: David Maness
Assistant Managing Editors: Dale M. Brown
(planning), George Constable, George G. Daniels
(acting), Martin Mann, John Paul Porter
Art Director: Tom Suzuki
Chief of Research: David L. Harrison
Director of Photography: Robert G. Mason
Senior Text Editor: Diana Hirsh
Assistant Art Director: Arnold C. Holeywell
Assistant Chief of Research: Carolyn L. Sackett
Assistant Director of Photography: Dolores A. Littles

Chairman: Joan D. Manley
President: John D. McSweeney
Executive Vice Presidents: Carl G. Jaeger,
John Steven Maxwell, David J. Walsh
Vice Presidents: Nicholas Benton (public
relations), John L. Canova (sales),
Nicholas J. C. Ingleton (Asia), James L. Mercer
(Europe/South Pacific), Herbert Sorkin
(production), Paul R. Stewart (promotion),
Peter G. Barnes
Personnel Director: Beatrice T. Dobie
Consumer Affairs Director: Carol Flaumenhaft
Comptroller: George Artandi

WORLD WAR II

Editorial Staff for *Red Army Resurgent*
Editor: Gerald Simons
Designer/Picture Editor: Raymond Ripper
Picture Editor: Josephine Burke
Text Editors: Brian McGinn, Robert Menaker
Staff Writers: Susan Bryan, Kumait Jawdat,
John Newton, Teresa M. C. R. Pruden
Chief Researcher: Oobie Gleysteen
Researchers: Charlie Clark, Kristin Baker,
Diane Bohrer, Marion F. Briggs, Mary G. Burns,
Frances R. Glennon, Elizabeth Hughes Weatherley
Art Assistant: Mary Louise Mooney
Editorial Assistant: Connie Strawbridge

Special Contributor:
Champ Clark (text)

Editorial Production
Production Editor: Douglas B. Graham
Operations Manager: Gennaro C. Esposito,
Gordon E. Buck (assistant)
Assistant Production Editor: Feliciano Madrid
Quality Control: Robert L. Young (director),
James J. Cox (assistant), Michael G. Wight
(associate)
Art Coordinator: Anne B. Landry
Copy Staff: Susan B. Galloway (chief),
Sheirazada Hann, Peter Kaufman, Victoria Lee,
Barbara F. Quarmby, Celia Beattie
Picture Department: Alvin L. Ferrell

Correspondents: Elisabeth Kraemer (Bonn);
Margot Hapgood, Dorothy Bacon, Lesley Coleman
(London); Susan Jonas, Lucy T. Voulgaris (New
York); Maria Vincenza Aloisi, Josephine du Brusle
(Paris); Ann Natanson (Rome). Valuable assistance
was also provided by: Martha Mader (Bonn); Pat
Stimpson (London); Felix Rosenthal (Moscow);
Carolyn T. Chubet, Miriam Hsia (New York); M. T.
Hirschkoff (Paris); Mimi Murphy (Rome); Bogdan
Turek (Warsaw).

The Author: JOHN SHAW, born and educated in
England, worked for British and Australian newspapers before joining *Time* in 1963 in Saigon. He
later served as a correspondent for *Time* in Los
Angeles, Rome, Jerusalem and the Soviet Union,
and as bureau chief in Moscow from 1972 to 1975.
Now living in Australia, he is a political correspondent and columnist for American and Asian newspapers and magazines.

The Consultants: COLONEL JOHN R. ELTING, USA
(Ret.), is a military historian and author of *The
Battle of Bunker's Hill, The Battles of Saratoga* and
Military History and Atlas of the Napoleonic Wars.
He edited *Military Uniforms in America: The Era
of the American Revolution, 1755-1795* and *Mili-
tary Uniforms in America: Years of Growth, 1796-
1851,* and was associate editor of *The West Point
Atlas of American Wars.*

EARL F. ZIEMKE, a research professor of history at
the University of Georgia, specializes in German
history and World War II. After wartime service as
a U.S. Marine in the Pacific, he received his Ph.D.
from the University of Wisconsin and worked as a
supervisory historian at the Department of the
Army in Washington, D.C. His books include *Stalingrad to Berlin: The German Defeat in the East,
The German Northern Theater of Operations* and
Battle for Berlin.

Library of Congress Cataloging in Publication Data

Shaw, John, 1931 (May 10)-
  Red Army resurgent.

  (World War II; 20)
  Bibliography: p.
  Includes index.
  1. World War, 1939-1945—Campaigns—Russia.
2. Russia (1923-   U.S.S.R.).   Armiia—History.
I. Time-Life Books.   II.   Title.   III.   Series.
DK264.S52   940.54'21   79-21867
ISBN 0-8094-2520-3
ISBN 0-8094-2519-X lib. bdg.

For information about any Time-Life
book, please write:

Reader Information
Time-Life Books
541 North Fairbanks Court
Chicago, Illinois 60611

CONTENTS

MAKING READY TO FIGHT AGAIN

n Kharkov, Wehrmacht troops consider stopping at the German-run Caucasus Café. German civilians opened many such businesses in the Ukraine.

A SPRINGTIME OF RISING GERMAN HOPES

On April 19, 1942, Helmut Pabst, a veteran German non-commissioned officer serving with an artillery unit on the Russian front, sent cheerful news to his parents and friends in Frankfort on the Main. "Yesterday I saw the first butterfly," he wrote with delight. "At midday I sat with the infantry boys on a tree trunk in the gully and stretched myself out in the sun."

Such were the restorative powers of spring for the more than 2.5 million Wehrmacht soldiers stretched along the 1,500-mile battlefront. The Germans, all-conquering the first six months of Hitler's most ambitious blitzkrieg, had been halted in December by the Russian winter and Soviet counterattacks; then, ill-clad and unaccustomed to defensive warfare, they had suffered three months of frostbite, hunger and despair. But as the spring thaw melted the frozen earth into a sticky gumbo, the Germans' spirits quickened. They had given up little territory of significance and Moscow was less than 100 miles away. From Hitler came assurances of more tanks and munitions, along with compliments for a "defensive success of unequaled magnitude." Hitler vowed that as soon as the muddy steppes dried out, the armies of the Third Reich would resume their mighty offensive and secure the final victory.

The Wehrmacht went to work. Bridges uprooted by ice floes were rebuilt. Corduroy roads were laid to reestablish supply routes. Soldiers' boots, rotted by snow and mud, were resoled or replaced. Fresh divisions arrived; battle-weary units moved to staging areas for rest and refitting.

During the weeks of preparation, there was time for pleasure. Lucky soldiers explored Kharkov, Poltava and other occupied towns. They drank beer and vodka in the local taverns, found compliant Russian women, acquired souvenirs in exchange for assorted loot they had taken from Soviet captives. And they talked eagerly of the coming campaign. "The thought of the spring offensive," said a German major, "means to the enlisted men that things will change. Things will be moving forward again. The 'good times of summer' are coming again."

Stationed in one of the remote sectors of the Russian front, a German soldier laden with combat gear waits for his marching orders on a spring afternoon.

A propaganda poster proclaims the Germans liberators of the Russians.

A German pilot in an observation plane buzzes along an endless file of captured Soviet troops, marching from the Moscow front to prison camps in the rear.

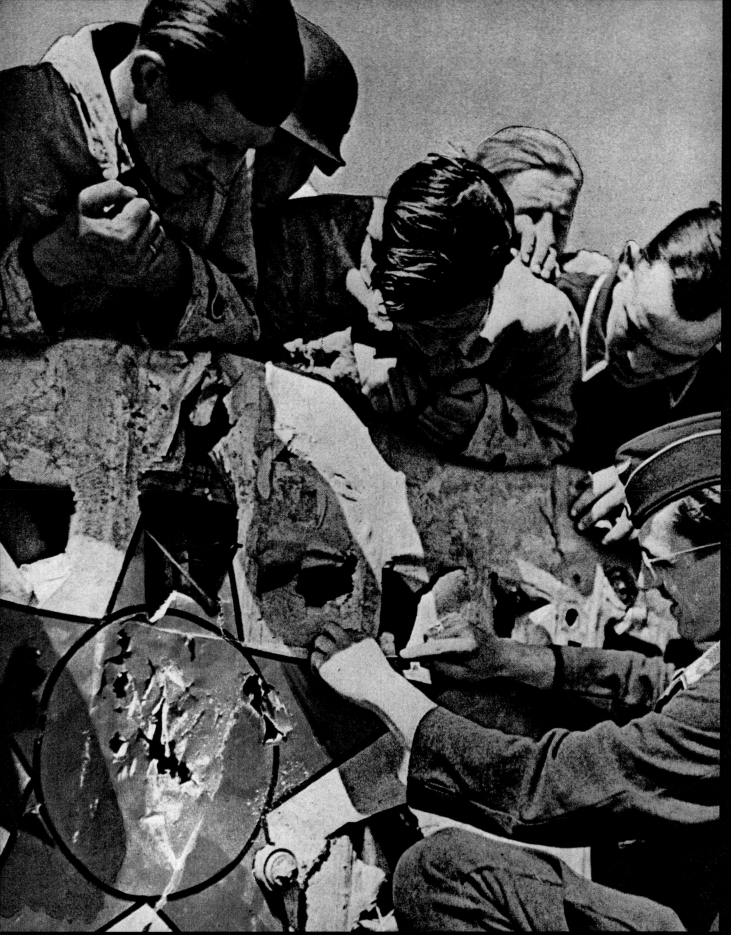

Souvenir-hunting antiaircraft gunners jubilantly peel the Red Army star from the fuselage of a Soviet bomber they brought down behind the battle front.

13

Moving up to the front in fair weather, a German supply convoy rumbles across a wooden bridge spanning the Vorskla River in the Ukrainian town of Poltava.

Battling the boggy Russian terrain, German motorcyclists struggle to extricate one of their machines from the mud. They finally pried it loose by using a

Germans unload a truck bearing artillery projectiles, whose propelling charges came separately in the wicker receptacles

pole from the pile at left.

On the Finnish front, a horse-drawn sled supplies the German outposts.

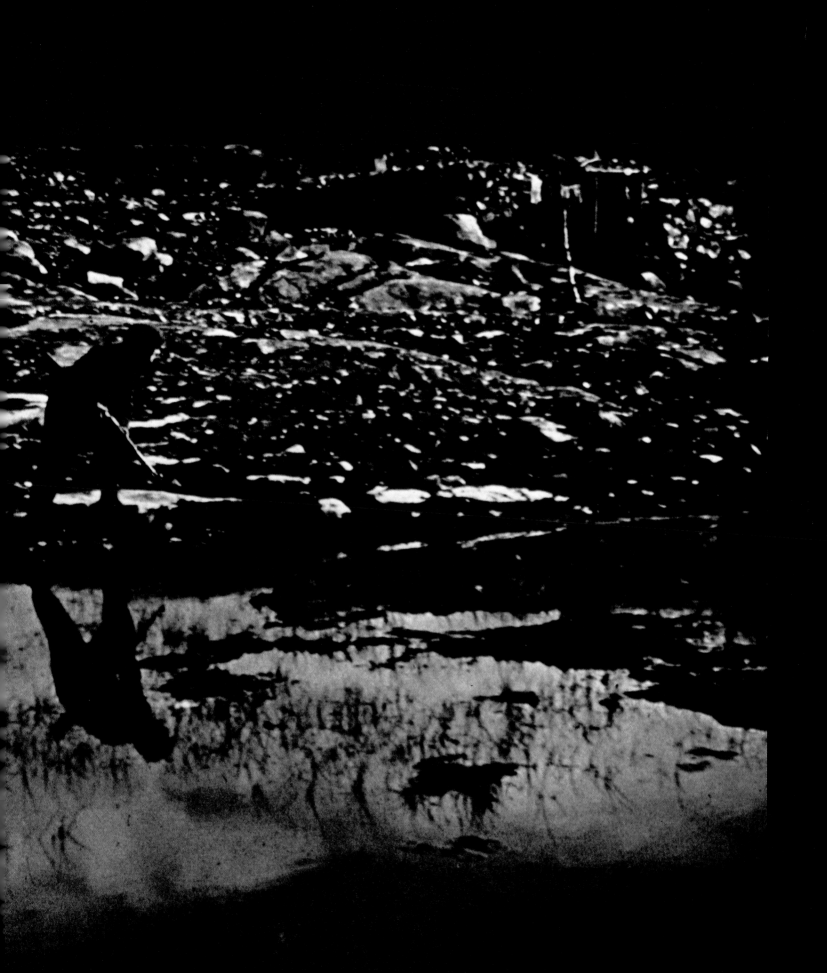

Heading across the forbidding Finnish tundra, Wehrmacht mountain troops on combat patrol pass a pool of meltwater on their way to probe Soviet defenses.

1

Josef Stalin greeted the new year, 1942, with grim determination and a strong hunch. Now was the time, his instincts told him, to launch his first strategic offensive of the War, and he had ordered Stavka—General Headquarters of the Soviet High Command—to prepare plans for major attacks at key points along the main battle front *(map, pages 24-25)*, which ran 1,500 miles from Leningrad on the Baltic Sea to Sevastopol on the Black Sea. To present the plan to his top advisers, Stalin scheduled a meeting for January 5 at his Kremlin quarters.

On the face of it, a Soviet offensive now was foolhardy at best. Since Hitler had launched his invasion on June 22, 1941, the Red Army had suffered a series of catastrophic defeats in battles whose colossal scale boggled the minds of the British and the Americans. At the Belorussian city of Minsk in June, German armies captured 300,000 Soviet troops, 2,500 tanks and 1,500 artillery pieces. In early August, the Germans took 103,000 prisoners, 300 tanks and 800 guns in the Uman region. At about the same time they bagged another 100,000 prisoners, 2,000 tanks and 1,900 guns at Smolensk. And these losses were topped in late August around Kiev, where the Germans captured more than 650,000 troops, nearly 900 tanks and 4,000 guns. In those four vast battles alone, the Red Army also lost one million men dead and wounded. In addition, the Soviet Union lost territory twice the size of Germany, much of its best agricultural land, a large part of its industry and a third of its population.

The worst crisis came in November, when German armies drove to within 10 miles of Moscow's city limits. Even the usually confident Stalin was a shaken man. In a telephone call to the commander of the front, General Georgy K. Zhukov, the dictator begged for a shred of hope: "Are you sure we are going to be able to hold Moscow? I am asking you this with an aching heart. Tell me honestly as a member of the party."

Zhukov replied yes, the capital would be held—if two more armies were made available. To this Stalin muttered, "I'm glad *you* are so certain."

The general was as good as his word. Bolstered by the two armies Stalin scraped up, Zhukov's battered forces stopped the Germans in December. Then they mounted a huge pincers movement to either side of the city, and by early

ANOTHER YEAR OF CALAMITY

January they had driven the Germans more than 75 miles west. It was this counterattack that inspired Stalin to call for his winter offensive.

Late on the evening of January 5, a sizable group of generals and high-ranking government officials arrived for the meeting in Stalin's office at the Kremlin. They immediately noticed a significant change in the decor, which suggested to them what the dictator had in mind. The familiar portraits of Marx and Engels had been taken down from their prominent places, and in their stead were hanging pictures of Suvorov and Kutuzov—Russian heroes who had fought in wars against the Turks and French.

First on the program was the Chief of the General Staff, Marshal Boris M. Shaposhnikov, a capable career officer who in 1918 had joined the "Workers and Peasants Red Army." Shaposhnikov sketched out an astonishing plan that he had concocted against his better judgment. Five large-scale offensives would be launched almost simultaneously. They would relieve Leningrad, which had been blockaded by the Germans since last September; would in twin attacks shove the Wehrmacht back on both sides of Moscow; would recapture the rich Donets basin in the Ukraine; and would drive the Germans out of the Crimean Peninsula on the Black Sea. These blows, supposedly, would put the Germans to flight out of the Soviet Union.

When Shaposhnikov had finished his presentation, Stalin spoke to dispel any doubts about what his own position was. "The Germans are in disarray as a result of their defeat at Moscow," he stated. "They are poorly fitted out for the winter. This is a most favorable time for the transition to a general offensive." Stalin then called on General Zhukov to express his opinion.

Zhukov, who always had strong opinions, said he was in favor of continuing his attacks on the Moscow front if sufficient troops and tanks could be supplied, but he pronounced the other operations much too ambitious for the men and matériel on hand. "Without powerful artillery support," he asserted, "they will be ground down and suffer heavy—not to say unjustifiable—losses."

General Zhukov's position was backed by Nikolai A. Voznesensky, the outspoken Chairman of the State Planning Commission and the chief mobilizer of Soviet war production, which was just now beginning to turn out tanks and planes in significant numbers. Voznesensky declared that there would not be enough matériel to supply all of the operations that had been proposed.

Stalin shrugged off the objections and said impatiently, "We must grind the Germans down with all possible speed, so that they cannot attack in the spring." This explanation was heartily endorsed by Georgy M. Malenkov, a top political commissar, and NKVD chief Lavrenty P. Beria, whose secret-police force was virtually an independent state within the Soviet state. They accused Voznesensky of making mountainous obstacles out of molehill problems.

Stalin asked for any further comments. There were none. "So," he said, "this, it seems, ends the discussion."

Discussion? Nothing had been discussed, and Zhukov said as much to Shaposhnikov as the meeting broke up. Marshal Shaposhnikov agreed. "It was foolish to argue," he said. "The Boss had already decided. The directives have gone out to almost all of the fronts, and they will launch the offensive very soon."

"Well then, why did Stalin ask me to give my opinion?" growled Zhukov.

"I just don't know, old fellow," Shaposhnikov replied with a sigh, "I just don't know."

But both men did know: The meeting had been another of Stalin's charades, designed to key up the generals and remind them that he called the turns. As for Stalin's plan, no one present that night—not even Stalin himself—genuinely believed that the tide of battle could be turned that year, much less in a winter of desperate preemptive attacks. In fact, these attacks would fall far short of their objectives and make it considerably easier for the Germans to resume their offensive in the spring.

Yet the tide-turning battle on the Russian front—the battle that Winston Churchill later called "the hinge of fate" on which World War II swung in the favor of the Allies—would indeed be fought in 1942, and in a place that on January 5 seemed quite safe from the Germans. The place was Stalingrad on the Volga River, a modest industrial city then 300 miles behind the battle front.

At Stalingrad in August, the Russians and the Germans would clash in an apocalyptic battle that engaged upward of four million soldiers. Both sides suffered a total of 1.5

million casualties, earning Stalingrad the grisly name of "Verdun on the Volga." And in the heat of that battle, the Red Army would be forged from scrap iron into steel.

Stalin's offensive was scheduled to begin on January 10, so his commanders had precious little time for preparation. It made no real difference. The Red Army was still patently inferior to the Wehrmacht in almost every category, and since it was fighting on raw courage and sheer manpower (six million men in spite of all losses), it was as ready for battle now as it would be in the near future.

From top to bottom, the Red Army was disastrously short of able leaders. At the command level, this was in large part the bitter heritage of the Great Purge of the late 1930s, when Stalin, in an epic fit of paranoia at the Army's growing power and independence, executed or imprisoned more than 35,000 career officers of all ranks. Many of the senior officers who survived had better credentials as Stalin loyalists than as competent commanders.

Good, bad or indifferent, the officer corps was decimated during the early German victories, and the survivors were handicapped even more by the political commissar system, which saddled field commanders with coequal Communist Party watchdogs who were empowered to veto their orders even under combat conditions. Many a disobedient or faltering commander was shot on the spot by his commissar.

The enlisted ranks, too, were a shambles. The Red Army had suffered crippling early losses among the educated technicians and self-starting noncoms needed to make a modern army work. The great mass of men were still only sketchily trained; some could hardly operate their own personal weapons, which were in short supply as well. Most of the troops were peasants and workers from remote sections of the immense country. They had a natural tendency to flock together on the battlefield, which made them splendid targets. The Soviet soldiers were fond of quoting an old saying: "It is better to die in company, and Mother Russia has sons enough." When the Russians fought as individuals they ordinarily fought well, but soldiers they were not—at least not yet.

In the beginning, the Red Army's elemental response to its crushing defeats was to break down into a primitive form of military organization—the rifle brigade that numbered a few thousand infantrymen assembled from shattered units and thrown into battle under the command of recently promoted colonels and majors. Tactically, these scratch outfits were disastrous. One unit, for example, was not even able to support its few remaining tanks to exploit a local breakthrough; the soldiers just stood around watching the action, and when the tanks were knocked out because of the infantry's failure to silence the Germans' antitank guns, the men simply wandered off as if in a daze.

A MODERN-DAY IVAN THE TERRIBLE

In training, Soviet infantrymen edge across a log.

The Red Army possessed only one secret weapon: the Soviet infantryman. The Germans, lulled by the success of their early blitzkriegs, were not prepared for the tenacity and ferocity with which the "Ivans" fought at Moscow and all during the winter of 1941-1942. Indeed, as the War went on, many a Wehrmacht trooper found himself struggling with an almost superstitious fear of his counterpart.

"In the evenings," wrote one German, "we used to talk of the end. Some slit-eyed Mongol was waiting for each of us. Sometimes all that mattered was that our bodies should get back to the Reich, so that our children could visit the graves."

Certainly there was little in the appearance of the Red Army Infantryman to inspire such terror. He wore a shapeless tunic belted over his trousers; his winter boots were more often made of felt than leather. He wore a forage cap in summer and one with ear flaps in winter, and it was only later in the War that he enjoyed a steel helmet. Instead of socks, he was issued long flannel strips that were carefully wrapped about the feet and ankles.

Ivan suffered for weeks on end without hot food, subsisting on cold cooked grain, salt fish and hardtack. When the field kitchens did catch up with him, they had little more to dispense than cabbage soup and tea.

But his peasant background made him at home on the land, he took easily to military training, and he was possessed of a terrible determination to beat back the invaders. The Germans found him to be a master of entrenchment. "When the Russian has dug himself into his native soil he is a doubly dangerous opponent," said a German officer. He called the Soviet infantry "willing, undemanding, suitably trained and equipped, and above all brave and endowed with a self-sacrificing devotion to duty." The ultimate compliment came from German Field Marshal Ewald von Kleist: "The men were first-rate fighters from the start. They became first-rate soldiers with experience."

The only maneuver at which the riflemen excelled was the reckless, flat-out charge: In wave upon tragic wave, they ran straight ahead into German gunfire. The suicidal charge became an officially accepted tactic; men were spent as freely as ammunition in wearing down the Germans by massive attrition. A Soviet staff officer put it bluntly: "We have a superiority in potential manpower. We've got to translate that superiority into terms of slaughter. And that won't be too difficult. Russians have a contempt for death. If we can keep them armed, the Germans will leave their own corpses scattered all over the steppes."

In spite of all its deficiencies, the Red Army did have certain advantages for the winter offensive. As Stalin had remarked, the Germans were shaken by their failure to capture Moscow, and they were ill-prepared to face the cruel Russian winter, with its chest-high snowdrifts and temperatures that plunged as low as −50° F. The invasion had been cockily planned to end by autumn, and greatcoats and fur-lined boots had been ordered only for the 60 divisions expected to remain on occupation duty.

The rest of the Wehrmacht suffered horribly from frostbite, and to combat the cold the soldiers wore layered assortments of tablecloths, towels and whatever else they could find. They became "Winter Fritzes"—clownlike figures in the Soviet press. The Red Army forces were more warmly dressed, and they knew that winter was their ally.

Moreover, the Germans often went hungry; their supply lines were long, and food shipments had low priority. Even with meals before them, the numb-fingered soldiers found that eating was painful and frustrating. A hot meal would freeze before it could be consumed. A German officer reported that: "One man who was drawing his ration of boiling soup at a field kitchen could not find his spoon. It took him 30 seconds to find it, but by then the soup was lukewarm. He began to eat it as quickly as he could, without losing a moment's time, but already the soup was cold, and soon it would be solid."

Unknowingly, the Russians had another asset: Adolf Hitler. The Führer, cosseted in his Wolf's Lair headquarters in the Rastenburg forest of East Prussia, meddled in military affairs as persistently as Stalin did, though heretofore with better effect. Just as Stalin's command to stand fast had led to the enormous Soviet entrapments at Kiev and elsewhere, so Hitler in December had ordered most of his armies to hold at all cost—despite his generals' recommendation of a strategic retreat to consolidate their lines.

"The troops must dig their nails into the ground," Hitler had said. "They must dig in and not yield an inch." Above all, there was to be absolutely no retreat from Moscow. On this point the Führer was so rigid and splenetic that when General Heinz Guderian withdrew his 2nd Panzer Group a

Soviet infantrymen lie sprawled in heaps, dead where they fell in one of their typical headlong charges 200 miles to the south of Leningrad during the winter of 1941-1942. One German was astonished to see the Russians "climbing with complete indifference and cold-bloodedness over the bodies of hundreds of fallen comrades in order to take up the offensive from the same spot."

Norway

Barents Sea

• Murmansk

Sweden

White Sea

• Archangel

GULF
OF
BOTHNIA

Finland

Baltic Sea

Hango •

LAKE
LADOGA

URAL MOUNTAINS

Ob River

GULF OF FINLAND

• Volkhov

Leningrad

Tikhvin

Irtysh

LAKE ILMEN

Staraya Russa

Demyansk •

Volga

Kholm •

LAKE SELIGER

River

Poland

Rzhev

Sverdlovsk •

Iset River

Vitebsk •

• Smolensk

• Moscow

• Yelnya

Oka River

Minsk •

B E L O R U S S I A

Roslavl •

• Tula

Volga

Chelyabinsk •

Mius River

Tobol River

Dnieper River

• Gomel

• Belev

River

Kuibyshev •

• Magnitogorsk

Orel •

Desna River

Don River

Kursk •

JANUARY 7, 1942

• Voronezh

Kiev •

Oskol River

Union of

Kharkov •

Kalach •

Socialist

Poltava •

Krasnograd •

• Kupyansk

Serafimovich •

Uman •

Dnieper

Izyum •

Bairak

• Kletskaya

Chir River

River

UKRAINE

Donets River

Stalingrad

Zaporozhye •

Ural River

Rumania

Stalino •

Don   River

• Kotelnikovo

Volga River

Odessa •

CRIMEA

Sea of Azov

C A U C A S U S

• Elista

Aral Sea

Sevastopol •

Belaya Glina •

Feodosia

Kerch

Maikop •

• Armavir

Syr Darya

Parpach

• Tuapse

Mozdok •

Terek   River

Bulgaria •

MOUNT
ELBRUS

• Grozny

Black Sea

CAUCASUS MOUNTAINS

Caspian
Sea

Amu Darya River

Turkey

• Batumi

Baku •

| 0 | 100 | 200 | 300 | 400 | 500 |

Scale of Miles

Iran

SIBERIA

• Tomsk

Ob River

Novosibirsk

Soviet
Republics

LAKE BALKHASH

Alma-Ata •
LAKE ISSYK-KUL

River

China

Tashkent •

• Samarkand

Afghanistan   India

short distance southwest of Moscow, Hitler sacked his best panzer commander. Others had followed as the Führer settled his long-standing feud with the arrogant, opinionated Prussian officer corps. Field Marshal Walther von Brauchitsch, Commander in Chief of the Army, had resigned in ill health, and Hitler officially took over the vacated post, which in fact he had held for several months. To his generals Hitler bragged, "Anyone can do the little job of directing operations in the War."

The disposition of German forces on the Moscow front was fully as important as Hitler believed. Here the Wehrmacht was in greatest danger. And it was here that Stalin launched his first and strongest counterattack.

The Moscow offensive persevered with the two-pronged attacks inaugurated by General Zhukov in December. To the north, two Soviet armies attacked toward Demyansk and three more armies attacked toward Belev to the south and east. These drives by 76 divisions quickly produced a large irregular bulge in the German lines and threatened to isolate the German Ninth Army in the Rzhev area. To the south of Moscow, even larger Soviet forces struck due west in the general direction of Smolensk, but here the going was tougher. Surrounded German units expertly formed circular hedgehog defenses to protect themselves against attack from any direction. They held their ground and kept busy Soviet units that otherwise could have advanced farther to the west and south.

Week after week, continuous fighting raged the length and breadth of the enormous Moscow front. The battles were particularly fierce in the north around Demyansk, Kholm and Staraya Russa; if Soviet forces broke through there, they might link up with armies that began attacking southward from the Leningrad sector on January 13. Red Army units did penetrate to the center of Staraya Russa, blowing up ammunition dumps and reducing the ancient trading post to rubble. But the German 2nd Corps, surrounded in a 20-by-40-mile hedgehog between Demyansk and Kholm, held out through a two-and-a-half-month siege with the aid of supplies flown in by the Luftwaffe.

Soviet forces, too, were surrounded in great swirling battles around Vyazma, in the center of the Moscow front between the two enormous pincers. The Germans cut off

By January 7, 1942, the Wehrmacht had conquered more than 500,000 square miles of the Soviet Union and confronted the Red Army along an immense front (red line) extending from the Barents Sea in the north to the Black Sea in the south. Moscow was still being threatened by German forces less than 100 miles to the west; Leningrad remained surrounded; and Sevastopol, in the Crimea, was under siege. Hitler had decided that his primary target would be the rich oil fields of the Caucasus. But neither side guessed, as the new year began, that the great battle on which the war would hinge would be fought at Stalingrad, a modest industrial city on a bend of the Volga River 300 miles behind the present front lines.

General P. A. Belov's cavalry corps and three divisions of the Thirty-third Army under Lieut. General M. G. Yefremov. For weeks the Russians hung on and fought back. Belov's horsemen finally sliced through to Soviet lines, but Yefremov and most of his men were blocked at every turn. Severely wounded and facing capture, Yefremov shot himself.

Elsewhere, the Soviet attacks fared poorly. The armies in the Leningrad sector failed to break through to the besieged city, and one army was surrounded on boggy terrain to the south. Far to the south of the Moscow front, Soviet forces did manage to drive a salient into the German lines near Izyum, but they could advance no farther and were left in a dangerously exposed position. At the extreme southern end of the front, Soviet forces attempted to relieve German pressure on besieged Sevastopol by making an amphibious assault on the nearby Kerch Peninsula jutting out into the Black Sea. The expedition proved to be a costly failure. The Sevastopol garrison attempted to break out of the encircling German lines, but it too came a cropper.

Nevertheless, Stalin stopped at nothing to keep his offensives going. He juggled his commanders and shifted whole armies about, sometimes for no apparent purpose. On the Moscow front, he deprived Zhukov of the First Shock Army just when the general needed it most, and only to place it in reserve. Zhukov objected vigorously, saying that he had earmarked that army for his attack toward Vyazma. "Don't protest," Stalin retorted. "Send it along. You have plenty of troops—just count them."

And so it was that, in late February, Stalin's much-vaunted general offensive ran out of steam and presently ground to a halt, just as reasonable Soviet officers had said it would on January 5. The Red Army had won isolated chunks of relatively unimportant terrain and had been gravely weakened in the process.

General Zhukov indulged himself a dry recapitulation: "Stalin was very attentive to advice but, regrettably, sometimes took decisions not in accord with the situation."

Yet the winter campaign had not been much of a victory for the Germans either. German casualties amounted to nearly 200,000 men, and only by dint of skillful and courageous fighting had Hitler's Wehrmacht been able to hold—in roughly the same position that the generals had hoped to occupy in the strategic withdrawal forbidden by the Führer.

This fact, of course, escaped Hitler's notice. He heartily agreed with Propaganda Minister Joseph Goebbels, who put out word that "the Führer alone saved the Eastern Front this winter." Goebbels noted credulously in his diary, "The Führer described to me how close we were to a Napoleonic winter. Had he weakened for one moment, the front would have caved in—a catastrophe that would have put the Napoleonic disaster far into the shade."

Spring was a godsend for both exhausted foes. The Russian *rasputitsa*—the spring thaw—worked its way north, turning the steppes into seas of mud and mercifully curtailing large-scale operations. Now was the time for both the Red Army and the Wehrmacht to prepare for the really serious fighting—in the summer campaigns.

Hitler had been working on plans for these campaigns when he was so rudely interrupted by Stalin's winter offensive. And now, with his command situation presumably straightened away by the firing of more than 30 disappointing generals, he proceeded to plan zealously for the happy days when the mud dried up. Then he would have his kind of weather—panzer weather, Luftwaffe weather.

At first Hitler had proposed to call his 1942 offensive Operation *Siegfried* for the legendary Teutonic hero. However, mature thought revealed to him the mixed results of his pretentiously named 1941 invasion plan, Operation *Barbarossa*—so called after the 12th Century Holy Roman Emperor—and he settled for a more modest name, Operation *Blau* (Blue).

But except for the name there was nothing modest about *Blau*; it was an operation grandiose in the extreme. The main feature of *Blau* was a strike in overwhelming strength into the oil-rich Caucasus, with the northern anchor of the drive to be established at a place of secondary importance, Stalingrad. Ultimately, Hitler saw the entire southern campaign as the left prong of a gigantic pincers movement. The right prong was to be General Erwin Rommel's Afrika Korps, which would capture Tobruk, eliminate the British forces in Egypt and go on to greater things.

Rommel would take the Arabian oil fields and lance through the Middle East to link up with Wehrmacht forces slashing south through the Caucasus Mountains to the Turkish border. The Turks had 26 divisions stationed on their

TWO SURGICAL [...] THAT [...]

The first attempt [...]
February 1942 [...]
units were [...]
northwest [...]

At Demyansk [...]
mancheld [...]
ing one 100 [...]
by Junkers [...]
where [...]
planes had [...]
lines and on [...]
tied handfuls [...]

Ultimately, both [...]
the successful [...]
they led Hitler [...]
mount the aims [...]
grander scale at Stalingrad [...]

Parachutes [...]

27

Soviet border, and Hitler expected that Turkey would join the War on the Axis side. Once these objectives were met, the Führer envisioned the construction of an East Wall—a "giant line of defense" that would seal off all of his immense colonial conquests for leisurely exploitation. He believed that the Soviet Union would simply drop out of the War once it had lost the Caucasus; and he felt that with the Russians knocked out, the Western Allies would prove amenable to a negotiated peace. After all, he would have defeated the Bolsheviks in the best interests of the Allies as well as the Reich.

Hitler personally took charge of planning Operation *Blau* in every detail, from logistics down to tactical operations at the division level. His work progressed rapidly in March but not, of course, without the usual irksome sounds from cautious generals and chronic complainers who found fault with his every imaginative scheme. These pettifoggers were of the opinion that Operation *Blau* was far too ambitious for the Wehrmacht and for the German economy. Hitler listened, but only from time to time.

Lieut. General Walter Warlimont, chief of the OKW (High Command of the German Armed Forces) National Defense Section, had a great deal to say. "Our war potential is lower than in the spring of 1941," he stated. Warlimont backed his judgment with figures. Of the 162 German divisions on the Russian front in March, eight were deemed ready for any mission, 47 were able to take part in a limited offensive, another three could undertake offensive operations after rest and rehabilitation, 73 could be expected to hold a defensive position, 29 could participate in limited defensive operations, and two divisions were unfit to do fighting of any kind. Furthermore, Warlimont summed up, the heavy losses in the winter fighting "cannot be made good" because Hitler had assigned all available reinforcements to other fronts. All together, the Army was short 625,000 troops.

As it happened, Hitler acknowledged the troop shortage and endorsed any reasonable attempt to improve the situation. He authorized General Walter von Unruh to comb the rear echelons and make transfers to the Russian front. Unruh, who came to be known as General *Heldenklau*, or Hero Snatcher, managed to dredge up an unspecified number of troops. Another 51 divisions were exacted from Germany's allies—Rumania, Italy, Hungary, Slovakia and even "neutral" Spain, which sent an understrength division of "volunteers." Most of these auxiliary forces were poorly trained and equipped, and the German High Command considered them useless for offensive purposes. But as guard units on quiet flanks they would free German forces for the attack.

These measures still left the Wehrmacht considerably short of sufficient strength, so the Army resorted to some statistical sleight of hand. Infantry divisions were reduced from nine battalions to seven, and companies from 180 soldiers to 80. The new divisions thus formed brought the Wehrmacht's strength up to an acceptable level—on paper.

In the matter of weaponry and equipment, Hitler faced a problem he could blame on no one but himself. In July of 1941, the Führer had been so confident of a quick victory over the Soviet Union that he had ordered cutbacks in war production for the Wehrmacht and had given priority to the production of U-boats and planes for the attack against Great Britain. During the winter fighting he had ordered a shift back to tanks and guns, but the change had come too late to get weapons into the pipeline for Operation *Blau*.

28

German forces would have to begin the offensive with only 7,500 new trucks, personnel carriers and other assorted vehicles to replace 75,000 similar vehicles that had been lost during the winter campaign. There was also a critical shortage of horses: 180,000 pack and draft animals had fallen victim to cold, overwork and the butcher's knife, and only 20,000 were sent to replace them.

Furthermore, to bolster Operation *Blau* in the south, armored units on the northern and central fronts would have to provide many tanks; divisions with a normal strength of 150 panzers were required to give up all but 40 or 50 tanks.

The Luftwaffe also was far below its best fighting strength, with only about half the number of serviceable aircraft it was supposed to have. For this, Hitler could at least put the blame on the man who was fast becoming his favorite scapegoat. Reich Marshal Hermann Göring, commander of the Luftwaffe, was in charge of the aircraft industry, which, according to one high-ranking German, "was like its boss, fat and incompetent." Göring insisted on controlling aircraft procurement, but he was too busy living well in Berlin to ensure that enough planes were produced. Thanks to poor administration and obsolete methods of production,

German factories had produced only 10,000 combat planes in 1941 and would produce only 4,000 more in 1942—not nearly enough to keep pace with ever-increasing losses in the east and west.

Ultimately, German industry could have filled all of the military shortages—if it had been put on a full wartime footing. But as Albert Speer, chief of war production and armaments, later pointed out, "Hitler demanded far less from his people than Churchill or Roosevelt did from their nations. The discrepancy between the total mobilization of labor forces in democratic England"—and in the Communist Soviet Union, he should have added—"and the casual treatment of this question in authoritarian Germany is proof of the regime's anxiety not to risk any shift in the popular mood. The German leaders were not disposed to make sacrifices themselves or to ask sacrifices of the people." As late as April 1942, German consumer-goods industries were producing only 3 per cent less than in peacetime.

Speer estimated that he needed another million workers to increase production for the new offensive and beyond. At the same time General Fritz Fromm, chief of the replacement army, was asking that 600,000 workers be pulled from

A skyline of oil derricks rises along the Caspian coast at Baku, the Soviets' main producing area and Hitler's primary objective during the Caucasus campaign of 1942. In 1941 enough crude oil was produced in Baku and the wells at Maikop and Grozny to satisfy most of the Soviet Union's needs, and the Führer insisted that unless he deprived the Russians of their main source he "would have to pack up the war."

the factories and put in uniform. Speer blamed the "arthritic" German bureaucracy for poor production, describing it as an "overbred, outmoded organization," unable to compete with the "organizationally simple methods and the art of improvisation" employed by the Americans and the Russians. But of course he said no such things to the Führer.

In his final concessions to reality, Hitler planned Operation *Blau* in stages, starting in May with enough time left to shift divisions and even armies from front to front and thus to use them in the main offensive in the summer. In two preliminary assaults, the Eleventh Army under General Erich von Manstein would clear Soviet forces from the Kerch Peninsula in the Crimea and finally capture besieged Sevastopol. On the Leningrad front, Army Group North would wipe out a Soviet pocket in the Volkhov swamps and if possible capture Leningrad itself. Hitler's most important pre-*Blau* attack was to be a drive by Army Group South to nip the big Soviet salient at Izyum. The Führer had originally intended to mount still other sizable attacks, but he gave them up to solidify *Blau*. To the surprise of his generals, he had even lost interest in the Moscow front—except for keeping it active enough to prevent Russian units there from peeling off and intervening in the south.

Simultaneously, in Moscow, Stalin was laying his own ambitious springtime plans. Far from being discouraged by his failed winter offensive, he found in it a dubious redeeming virtue; the Red Army's casualties had been much less severe than during Hitler's 1941 blitzkrieg. What is more, the shortage of troops that had halted the Soviet winter campaign was easily corrected by bringing up fresh divisions from the copious reserves of Russian cannon fodder. Ready and eager to attack again, Stalin convened a strategy meeting in the Kremlin in the last week of March.

Among those present were Stavka chief Shaposhnikov, by now toil-worn and ready to retire; Lieut. General Aleksandr M. Vasilevsky, who would soon succeed Shaposhnikov, and whose patient, plodding ways had a calming influence on his agitated colleagues; General Zhukov, the savior of Moscow; Marshal Kliment E. Voroshilov, a mediocre commander but an old drinking companion of Stalin's; and Marshal Semyon K. Timoshenko, who in 1940 had finally managed—using more than one million Red Army troops—to defeat

the 200,000-man army of little Finland, which had brazenly refused Soviet demands for portions of its territory.

Before Stalin got down to serious business, he casually dropped a large piece of bad news: The Western Allies were not going to open a second front in Europe in 1942. The Americans, he said, had now been at war for nearly four months, but they had been deplorably slow in gearing up their military, and they had yet to begin sending combat-ready divisions to Britain for a cross-Channel assault on the Continent. The British, meanwhile, were heavily committed in Egypt and Southeast Asia, and were none too eager for an invasion. Stalin would keep pressing the Allies to speed up their stockpiling of men and matériel for the second front, but there was no reasonable expectation of large-scale landings in France until the spring of 1943.

Having deepened his generals' gloom, Stalin gave the floor to Shaposhnikov. The marshal had scarcely begun his presentation when it became painfully clear that this was to be a rerun of the January 5 meeting. Shaposhnikov again announced—against his better judgment—a series of major attacks at key points all along the front. They were exactly the same five points, in fact, with two new ones thrown in for good measure.

Now opinions were called for, and of course Zhukov had one. He again advocated a heavy attack along his Moscow front, and again argued against spreading the Red Army's available resources too thin to be effective anywhere. Let him, Zhukov, attack west of Moscow, and let the rest of the front put up an active defense.

Stalin retorted angrily, "We cannot remain on the defensive and sit on our hands until the Germans strike first! We must strike on a broad front and probe the enemy's intentions." The dictator then described Zhukov's proposals as "half-measures."

Marshal Timoshenko was not in favor of half-measures either. He approved of preemptive strikes in general. In particular he liked the idea of a strike on Zhukov's front, to pin down German forces there, and he liked even more the idea of attacking on his own southern front, with the objective the city of Kharkov.

As usual, Stalin made the final decision—but this time, remarkably, he listened to the voices of moderation. The overblown plans Shaposhnikov had worked up for him would be extensively modified. In four areas where full-scale attacks had been called for, Soviet forces would put on "partial offensives"—which were different in certain unspecified ways from "half-measures" and from "active defenses." Stalin calculated that the main German attack of the summer would be directed toward Moscow from the south. To prepare for this eventuality, he ordered the bulk of the Red Army reserves to be stacked up in a blocking position around Voronezh, south of the Moscow front and north of Timoshenko's Izyum salient.

Only three Soviet offensives would be mounted. In the north and in the Crimea, armies would strike to lift the sieges of Leningrad and Sevastopol respectively. Most important, Timoshenko in May would burst out of his hard-won Izyum salient, drive northwest and recapture Kharkov, just as he had suggested. Kharkov was a prime strategic target. The fourth largest Soviet city, it stood at the confluence of two tributaries on the upper Donets River; it was also a road hub and an important commercial center.

Thus the major spring offensives planned by Stalin and Hitler put millions of men in collision courses in three sectors: on the Leningrad front; at Sevastopol in the Crimea; and especially around the Izyum salient southeast of Kharkov. Whatever happened at the opposite ends of the long front, the Izyum bulge was so close to the areas earmarked for *Blau* that the outcome there was bound to have an impact on Hitler's greatest offensive of the year.

At Leningrad, neither side succeeded in its designs for the isolated city. The German armies could not crack the stubborn Soviet defenses ringing Leningrad's southern outskirts, and, in fact, the line of battle changed very little. Soviet efforts to break through to the city were all but doomed by the plight of the Second Shock Army, whose 130,000 men had been cut off in the nearby Volkhov swamps since mid-March; rescue attempts diverted several Red Army divisions from their offensive assignments. At the end of March, a Soviet relief column managed to pierce the German lines and rush some supplies into the pocket. But the narrow corridor soon collapsed under German counterattack.

The Second Shock Army's prospects were bleak indeed, and its best hope seemed to be its new commander, Lieut. General Andrei A. Vlasov, a brilliant leader and popular hero who had flown in to take over on March 21. Vlasov had sprung to prominence during the disaster at Kiev, when his strong handling of an army made up of shattered divisions had been instrumental in preventing even greater losses. Then he had served with distinction in the winter counteroffensive in front of Moscow, and as soon as he arrived on the Volkhov front, he had shown his mettle by attacking two German divisions and advancing eight miles—to within 15 miles of Leningrad. It was true that his drive then petered out, but Moscow was still confident that if anyone could extricate the Second Shock Army, it was Vlasov.

But in April, Vlasov worked no miracles; his troops and tanks were immobilized by mud when the frozen swamps melted, and they could neither attack nor defend themselves. The crisis deepened in May, and two other armies in Vlasov's group launched another desperate drive to open an exit route through the surrounding German lines. Finally they succeeded in driving a 400-yard-wide corridor through to the Second Shock Army. Many of Vlasov's wounded were evacuated through the gap, and a large number of troops rushed out in wild disarray. The corridor remained open only for a short time, until German artillery and Luftwaffe dive bombers closed it.

In June, the men of the Second Shock Army were sick, starving, almost out of ammunition and under constant, heavy German fire. German forces kept closing in, reducing the pocket. Many a time Vlasov radioed for help, but each time the Leningrad front headquarters in charge of the Vlokhov area told him to keep on pressing the attack. At one point, headquarters sent a plane to get him out, but he refused to leave his men.

Finally, in late June, the pitiful remnants of the Second Shock Army made their last attempt to break out. The men punched two small holes in the German lines. Vlasov, having done all he could, ordered his survivors to destroy whatever heavy equipment remained, then break up into small groups to try to escape. Some men filtered out, but German troops swarmed over those still in the pocket. About 32,000 Russians survived to surrender; all the rest lay dead or dying in the putrid swamp. The debacle had cost the Red Army nearly 100,000 men.

As for Vlasov, his story took a weird turn. German soldiers came upon the hero general in a farmhouse and took him prisoner. When the Russians next heard of Vlasov, they

MURDER SQUADS ROAMING IN THE WEHRMACHT'S WAKE

Storming the eastern tip of the Crimea in the bleak last days of December 1941, Soviet forces came upon their first evidence of German atrocities on a massive scale. In and around the recaptured towns of the Kerch Peninsula, the Russians uncovered the bodies of thousands of slaughtered Jews—buried in ditches and shell craters or simply left where they fell.

The killings were the work of the *Einsatzgruppen*, special forces totaling 3,000 men, many from the SS, that swept across the U.S.S.R. behind the advancing German armies, with the express mission of executing all Jews. Otto Ohlendorf, the 34-year-old commander of the *Einsatzgruppe* that combed the Crimea, later testified that his men "would enter a village or city and order the prominent Jewish citizens to call together all Jews for the purpose of resettlement. The men, women and children were led to a place of execution. Then they were shot, kneeling or standing, and the corpses thrown into the ditch."

Searching for missing relatives, grieving Jewish survivors on the outskirts of Kerch peer at the corpses left behind by roving German killer squads.

Russian workers excavate a frozen ditch used for a mass burial.

were bewildered and mortified to find out that he had turned traitor and was leading an army of Soviet defectors against their homeland.

What had gone wrong with Vlasov? Soviet propagandists lamely suggested that he had been a German agent from the start and had deliberately led his army to destruction. Actually, Vlasov's harrowing experience convinced him that he had to undertake a patriotic war to liberate his countrymen from the ruinous clutches of Stalinism. But he paid the price for treason in full. In the last days of the War, when Vlasov and his anti-Communist Russians were stationed in Czechoslovakia, the turncoat general surrendered to American forces. He was sent back to the Soviet Union, where he was formally tried for treason, condemned and executed.

In May, while Vlasov's army still had a remote chance to survive, the situation far to the south—below the tense but static Moscow front—was nearing the explosion point in and around the Izyum salient. Under operational orders issued by Hitler on April 5, Army Group South under Field Marshal Fedor von Bock was preparing to attack the base of the Russian-held bulge from two directions; the Sixth Army, coming down from the north, was to link up with the First Panzer Army driving up from the south, thus bagging all the Soviet troops inside the salient. This operation, code-named *Fridericus,* was set to begin on May 18.

Simultaneously, however, Marshal Timoshenko was massing Soviet units in the salient for his big drive to capture Kharkov. These forces included 640,000 men and 1,200 tanks—the lion's share of the Red Army's armor. Timoshenko was scheduled to spring his attack on May 12, six days before Bock's. In such situations, the advantage normally went to the force that struck first.

Timoshenko struck first right on schedule and immediately made marvelous headway. In the north, his Twenty-first, Twenty-eighth and Thirty-eighth Armies made contact with units of the German Sixth Army and began driving them westward in heavy fighting. In the south, Timoshenko's Ninth Army, aided by his Sixth Army, drove back six German and Rumanian divisions and threatened Krasnograd, a rail center 60 miles southwest of Kharkov. By May 17, Soviet forces in the north were within 12 miles of Kharkov. Various Soviet units had spread 70 miles in just five days, and in

Berlin, a radio analyst viewed the situation with such concern that he prefaced a broadcast with the phrase, "Even if the Russians succeed in capturing Kharkov. . . ."

But the Soviet commanders were equally concerned, and with better cause. They were way out on a limb; vanguard units had outrun their supply lines. To make these matters worse, German soldiers captured in the south had been identified as belonging to a number of unreported panzer divisions. These panzers appeared to be gathering for a counterattack, although they were actually assembled for the German *Fridericus* offensive. Whatever the case, they were patently dangerous.

Among the Soviet officers who claimed to have scented trouble was Timoshenko's political commissar, a bouncy, bellicose man named Nikita S. Khrushchev, who would one day rise to the pinnacle of Soviet power. As Khrushchev later recalled, "We had broken through the enemy's front line of defense easily—too easily. We seemed to have a clear road ahead, deep into enemy territory. This was unsettling. It meant we had stumbled into a trap."

Timoshenko soon recognized the peril and, with Khrushchev's enthusiastic endorsement, ordered a halt to the offensive and began moving his armor and artillery around to face the panzers on his exposed left flank. "When all the necessary orders had been given and we had effectively shifted from the offensive to the defensive," Khrushchev continued, "I returned to my quarters to get some rest."

At 3 a.m. on May 18, as Khrushchev later recalled it, he was undressing for bed when he received an emergency visit from General Ivan K. Bagramyan, one of Timoshenko's more capable commanders. "I'm sorry to bother you, Comrade Khrushchev," the general burst out, "but I thought you should know that Moscow has countermanded our order halting the offensive."

"What?" cried Khrushchev. "How can this be? Who made the decision?"

"I don't know," replied Bagramyan. "All I know is that if we go ahead with the offensive, we'll be heading straight for disaster. Our troops in the salient will be doomed. I implore you: Speak to Comrade Stalin personally."

Instead, Khrushchev put through a call to Stavka and Lieut. General Aleksandr Vasilevsky, who had recently suc-

ceeded Marshal Shaposhnikov. "Aleksandr Mikhailovich," Khrushchev pleaded, "as a military man who had studied maps and who understands enemy strategy, you know the situation in greater detail than Comrade Stalin does. Please take a map along and explain to Comrade Stalin what will happen if we continue this operation."

Vasilevsky begged off, insisting that Stalin was out of touch at his *dacha*.

"Then go talk to him there," Khrushchev urged. "You know he'll see you any time. After all, there's a war going on. Take a map and show him how our decision to call off the offensive is the only rational thing to do."

"No," said Vasilevsky. "Comrade Stalin has already made up his mind. He has already issued his orders."

And that, as far as Vasilevsky was concerned, was that. "Anyone who has ever dealt with Vasilevsky," Khrushchev recalled later, "will be able to imagine the steady, droning voice with which he said this. I had no choice but to try to call Comrade Stalin myself. This was a very dangerous moment for me. I knew Stalin by now considered himself a great military strategist."

The telephone was answered not by Stalin but by Georgy Malenkov, one of Stalin's more sinister advisers. "I could hear Malenkov saying I was on the phone," wrote Khrushchev, "and asking Stalin to come talk to me. Malenkov came back and told me, 'Comrade Stalin says you should tell me what you want, and I'll pass on your message.' This was a sure sign of trouble."

As it happened, Khrushchev and Malenkov were deep-dyed enemies. Yet Khrushchev could only explain his difficulties, then wait uneasily while his rival reported to Stalin. The answer, when it came, was definitive. "There's no point in discussing it further," said Malenkov. "Stalin says the offensive must continue."

But the Germans had an offensive of their own mounted and ready to go. The Sixth Army—the northern arm of Field Marshal von Bock's pincers—had been driven out of position by the Soviet attack. But Bock decided to attack anyway with his southern arm, led by General Ewald von Kleist.

At dawn on May 18, after a thundering artillery prelude, Kleist drove forward on a wide front with eight infantry divisions, two panzer divisions and one motorized infantry division. He got behind the Russian tank column, and by nightfall his formations stood at the confluence of the Donets and Oskol Rivers at Izyum. In that single stroke, the Soviet corridor had been narrowed to 20 miles.

Meanwhile, the commander of the German Sixth Army, Lieut. General Friedrich Paulus, had made a neat maneuver while fighting desperate defensive battle: He managed to transfer his two panzer corps into an attacking position on his right. And on May 19, with the Soviet forces frantically turning south to meet Kleist's threat, the Sixth Army's tanks churned in to attack against the northern Soviet flank.

To prevent Paulus and Kleist from linking up, the Soviet commanders threw everything they had into the battle: men, tanks, guns, mines, felled trees—and dogs, hundreds of dogs. Huge packs of dogs, most of them Alsatians and Doberman pinschers, had been trained to run beneath enemy vehicles. On their backs the dogs carried explosive charges with trigger-rods that detonated on contact and blew up everything in the vicinity—including, of course, the dogs. German infantrymen soon learned to shoot every dog in sight, and the bomb-carrying canines did little damage.

Nothing the Soviets could throw against the Germans had much effect. On the afternoon of May 22, Kleist's 14th Panzer Division rolled into Bairak, on the northern bend of the Donets. Across the stream stood units from the Sixth Army, specifically, companies of the Viennese Hoch-und-Deutschmeister—a division named after a Teutonic Order. The Germans had joined hands, and the Russians were trapped within a circle of steel.

In their crazed efforts to break out, the Soviet forces stampeded. Primed by vodka and shouting "Ura! Ura!" ("Hurrah! Hurrah!"), they fell against the German lines with fists, bayonets and clubbed rifles. To no avail. The Soviet command admitted to 5,000 men killed, 70,000 missing and 300 tanks destroyed. In fact, about 200,000 Russians had trudged into German captivity, and the Soviet forces had lost most of their armor.

Surveying the wreckage of his armies during the final hours before the German linkup, Marshal Timoshenko exclaimed, "This is frightful!" Thereupon, without another word, he turned and left the field. Later, he tried to gather up fugitive survivors who had escaped the German pincers and found that he could lure them back only by setting up field kitchens. In absorbing yet another calamitous defeat, the Red Army had descended to a point where its main appeal was to its soldiers' hunger.

Small wonder Hitler gloated, *Der Russe ist tot!* ("The Russian is dead!"). With the Izyum salient his, he could now crowd it with troops and tanks for Operation *Blau*.

The Red Army had yet another opportunity for disaster—in the Crimea. After intermittent winter attacks on the Kerch Peninsula, Soviet forces there were beefed up with five armored brigades for Stalin's spring offensive. The Soviets attacked General von Manstein's Eleventh Army in April and learned to their distress that it too had been reinforced—by the fresh 22nd Panzer Division, the newly arrived Rumanian 7th Corps and the whole of the 8th Air Corps, with 21 fighter groups and plenty of Stuka dive bombers. Three days later, the Soviet offensive stopped dead.

Now Manstein could proceed to execute his own offensive as assigned by the Führer. He could quite easily eliminate the Soviet troops on the Kerch Peninsula and then terminate his lengthy siege of Sevastopol—all in time to take part in *Blau* operations in the Caucasus, just across the Black Sea from Sevastopol. Manstein's preparations for the Kerch attack were completed in early May. For some reason, he called the assault Operation *Bustard Hunt*, and in spite of the formidable Soviet defenses, the game-bird name would turn out to be quite felicitous.

On May 6, the general visited the front to have a look at the enemy defense line across an 11-mile-wide isthmus that joined the Kerch Peninsula and the main Crimean Peninsula. From a forward observation post of the 114th Artillery Regiment, he peered through binoculars at a great water-filled antitank ditch—16 feet deep, 11 yards wide—that ran from one side of the peninsula to the other and barred the way to the town of Kerch. Behind the ditch were countless land mines, barbed-wire obstacles and pillboxes. "That's where we've got to drive through," he told aides. "Good luck the day after tomorrow."

Operation *Bustard Hunt* began as scheduled on May 8. At 3:15 a.m., German artillery and Stukas provided cover for demolition teams, whose job it was to remove the land mines and cut through wire at the far edge of the ditch. The Russians answered with salvos of their own. Their positions had been placed for cross fire: All the gunners had to do was point their weapons out of their pillboxes and fire.

The first German attacks were driven back—precisely as Manstein planned. He had conspicuously deployed those units to suggest an attack eastward by his northern flank, and while Soviet defenders were looking north, German troops rode assault boats from the Black Sea right into the ditch from the south. The Russians were taken by surprise; and they never recovered.

Soon after that daring assault, German engineers had hung portable bridges over the ditch, and German infantrymen stormed across. Bustard-like, the Soviet defenders then took wing. Manstein's armored and motorized hunters took off in hot pursuit. "The defense was knocked off balance," admitted Major General Sergei M. Shtemenko, Deputy Chief of Stavka. "Troop control was lost and withdrawal eastward took place in disorder."

Some Soviet units desperately tried to hold back the German advance so that the other defenders could be ferried to the eastern side of the Kerch Strait in a kind of Russian Dunkirk. But by the 17th of May, more than 170,000 Soviet fighting men had been captured, along with 250 tanks and 1,100 artillery pieces. Mopping up continued apace. As Manstein pondered his easy victory, he wrote with feeling, "There was something unforgettable about this tempestuous chase. All the roads were littered with enemy vehicles, tanks and guns, and one kept passing long lines of prisoners."

The members of Stavka knew that this particular disaster was even worse than it seemed; it was largely due to egregious incompetence at the top level. One culprit was the Crimean front commander, Lieut. General D. T. Kozlov. Another was Deputy Defense Commissar Lev Z. Mekhlis, already infamous for cruelly humiliating generals. Soon after the German attack began, while Kozlov pottered around issuing useless orders, 21 Soviet divisions had been allowed to commit themselves piecemeal, leaving only two divisions in reserve. Mekhlis on May 8 sent an indignant message to Stalin blaming the whole mess on Kozlov.

To this Stalin answered angrily, "You are adopting the strange position of a detached observer who accepts no responsibility for the affairs of the Crimean front. That is a very comfortable position, but is one that absolutely stinks.

On the Crimean front, you are no detached onlooker but a responsible representative of Stavka—responsible for all the successes and failures of the front, and obliged to correct errors by the command on the spot."

Mekhlis also took a more active role in spreading confusion through the already panicky ranks. The specifics of his offenses came through in the form of another blast from Stalin: "If you had used assault aircraft not for auxiliary purposes but against the enemy's tanks and infantry, the enemy would not have broken through the front and the tanks would not have gotten through."

But there was blame enough for all, and Stalin distributed it with an even hand. Kozlov and his commissar were dismissed, and three other generals, including the air force chief who had cooperated with Mekhlis, lost their commands. Best of all, Mekhlis was fired as deputy defense commissar and moved to a minor noncombat post.

Meanwhile, the sorry misuse and reduction of the Soviet Crimean air force was greatly assisting General von Manstein as he shifted his forces toward Sevastopol. Manstein knew from long experience, however, that Operation *Sturgeon*—the final assault on the Black Sea fortress—would be a great deal more difficult than the Kerch Operation *Bustard Hunt*. The defenders had the Black Sea at their backs *(map, opposite)*, along with the guns of the Black Sea Fleet, and three heavily fortified lines ran in broad loops between them and Germans attacking from the north and east. It was a battle, Berlin admitted, in which advances could be measured "not by miles but by yards."

Ever since the Germans had first attacked the city in the fall of 1941, the Russians had defended it with fanatic determination. "If Sevastopol is destined to fall," Admiral I. S. Yumashev exhorted his troops, "it has to cost the Germans 100,000 men. If you force them to pay that price, your sacrifice will not be in vain."

The first German assault on October 30, 1941, had resulted in the taking of the Balaklava Hills. And it had produced the first of many Sevastopol heroes to be celebrated in Russian verse and song: the Five Sailors of Sevastopol. Their ammunition exhausted, each of the five men made bundles of their last grenades and flung themselves under onrushing German tanks, each man crippling a panzer. A second German attack in mid-December had pushed the defenders back to a line only five miles north of the city. But the operation had been halted on December 31, when German troops were rushed to the Kerch Peninsula to fight Soviet amphibious forces landing there in an effort to divert German troops from Sevastopol.

That winter, Sevastopol had become a bedlam of death dealt by ceaseless German artillery barrages and bombing raids. To escape the pounding, most of the citizens moved into underground shelters and caves surrounding the city, and there they set up factories that continued turning out arms and ammunition for the defenders. One factory was housed in vast cellars once used for a happier purpose: the storage of the famed Crimean champagne. Boris Voyetekhov, a *Pravda* correspondent who visited another factory, described a vast cellar "subdivided by heavy metal screens where hundreds of lathes hummed and rattled, producing mines." Conditions were makeshift. "A tractor motor generating electricity was puffing and smoking like an old samovar. On bunks that were built in three tiers along walls of the tunnels, the workers of other shifts slept. The strongest slept on top, where breathing was difficult. Below were the pale sallow children."

By drawing off German attackers, the Soviet landings at Kerch brought a measure of relief to the beleaguered Sevastopolians, and in January the people moved out of the caves, even though German guns were but five miles away. A mood of optimism gradually took hold in the next months until on May Day, recalled local party chief B. A. Borisov, "Everyone was talking about the Crimea being liberated and the siege lifted. Everyone was in an exalted holiday mood."

But 18 days later, the Germans had wiped out the Soviet forces on the Kerch Peninsula, and the people of Sevastopol trudged back into their caves, prepared for a new German onslaught. This time, they feared, the enemy would succeed. Soviet forces in the city had been bled white; the Luftwaffe had destroyed most of the Soviet ships bringing desperately needed supplies from the Caucasus on the eastern shores of the Black Sea.

By June 2, the Germans had brought up their heaviest artillery, including three massive fieldpieces originally designed to batter down France's Maginot Line. (The guns were not finished in time for that job, nor were they needed.) One of those giant guns was capable of lobbing its five-ton shell 29 miles. Far more practical for the purpose at hand were scores of hard-hitting 88mm antiaircraft guns.

The awful German bombardment began. For the next five days, a deadly rain of incendiary and explosive shells fell on the city. Soldiers and civilians died by the thousands.

By June 7, Manstein decided that he had softened up Sevastopol's defenses sufficiently to take the city by storm, and he so ordered. A wave of seven German and two Rumanian divisions attacked the first of the three lines of defense that protected the city: a zigzag, one to two miles deep, of trenches, tank obstacles and mines. The second

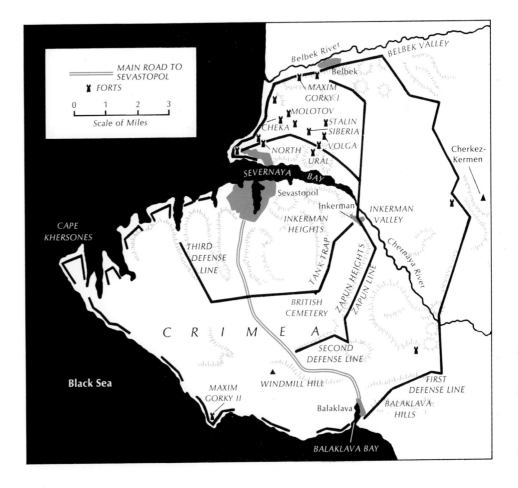

Sevastopol was protected from attacking German forces by three formidable lines of defense. The outermost line, some six to eight miles from the port, was a belt of strong points and minefields. Just to the rear, the second line was studded with machine-gun nests and was anchored on steel-and-concrete fortifications that guarded the northern approaches to Sevastopol. The last defense line, ringing the outskirts of the town, featured a wide antitank ditch and numerous pillboxes.

line, about a mile deep, had a string of heavy fortifications concentrated north of the city, and a section to the south known as the Zapun line. The German gunners nicknamed the forts Molotov, Stalin, Volga, Cheka and Siberia. Maxim Gorky I, the most imposing of the defenses, was more than 300 yards long and 40 yards deep, and mounted heavy 12-inch guns. (A similar fort, Maxim Gorky II, guarded the

southern approaches to the city.) If the invaders got past the forts to the north, they still had to cross Severnaya Bay, breach the Zapun line, and tackle the last ring of defense around the city: a maze of mortar pits, machine-gun posts and artillery emplacements.

It took the Germans two days to break through the first defense line and to begin attacking the forts. They concentrated first on Fort Stalin, capturing it on June 13. "This was probably the toughest enemy we ever encountered," read the battle report of the 22nd Infantry Division. The division took only four prisoners at Fort Stalin—and they surrendered only after their political commissar had killed himself.

To take Gorky I, whose guns controlled the Belbek Valley north of Sevastopol to the Black Sea—a distance of about three and one half miles—German gunners used Röchling "bombs," one-ton shells that burrowed through rock and concrete before they detonated. Two barrages of Röchlings cracked open Gorky's gun emplacements, enabling the Germans to take the battlements and batteries. Gorky was not dead, however. German sappers and infantrymen had to fight for every foot of the labyrinthine passages before they secured the ruined fort on June 17.

That same day, Molotov, Cheka, Siberia and Volga had been shelled and stormed into submission, as had the Ural Fort, the last bastion barring the advance of German and Rumanian units toward Severnaya Bay, which lay between them and Sevastopol. On June 20, the Germans charged the antiquated but nevertheless formidable North Fort, which dominated the entrance to the bay. The Russians filtered reinforcements into the fort from the sea in a hodgepodge armada of military and civilian craft to fight for a rail tunnel that led into the city. The Germans eventually took the tunnel and the fort, and were separated from the city only by narrow Severnaya Bay, 3,200 feet at its widest point.

At this point, the Germans had taken all of the second defense line, except for the southern Zapun fortifications. From his observation post on a cliff high above the city, Manstein took stock of the situation. "To the right was the city of Sevastopol," he later recalled, "and straight ahead a

A tremendous explosion destroys a Soviet munitions dump at Sevastopol on June 28, 1942, as the German Eleventh Army begins its final assault on the port city. The ammunition, stored in a fortified cave 90 feet high, had been blown up by fanatic defenders to make sure it would not fall into enemy hands; the blast killed thousands of homeless or wounded civilians who had taken refuge in chambers underneath the cave.

wall of cliff honeycombed with enemy positions." His plan was to outflank the heavily defended Zapun heights by breaking through at the line's northernmost point—the old Inkerman fortress.

On June 28, a German assault force crossed the Chernaya River east of the bay to assault the Inkerman. Inside the cliff was an arms factory, doing double duty as a haven for thousands of wounded and refugees.

Manstein's flanking movement proved to be unnecessary. "Just as our troops were entering the Inkerman," he wrote, "the whole cliff behind it shuddered under the impact of a tremendous detonation, and the 90-foot wall of rock fell in over a length of 900 yards, burying thousands of people beneath it." Rather than surrender, the Russians had blown themselves up.

With the Inkerman heights and valley taken, German assault boats swept across the bay under an umbrella of artillery and air support. On June 29, the Germans had breached the Zapun line, taken a cemetery for the British dead in the Crimean War of 1854-1856, and silenced the Soviet artillery batteries stationed among the shattered marble monuments. Then, rolling south from the Zapun line, the German 72nd Division took "Windmill Hill," and with it the main road into Sevastopol.

On July 1, the Germans began bombarding the inner city, for they wanted to avoid the losses they knew would come in house-to-house fighting. The Russians were forced to withdraw to Cape Khersones at the very western tip of the Crimea. Submarines evacuated the top military leaders and as many of the wounded as they could carry, while those left behind fought a desperate holding action against the advancing Germans. "We trust you to die here," one officer was told by a superior. "You will do this job and you will not get back alive. We are not trying to frighten you, but do not deceive yourself. The wounded are being withdrawn to Khersones. Cover them—until the last man, the last yard, the last breath."

The Russians continued to fight valiantly. "Whole masses of them rushed at our lines," recalled Manstein, "their arms linked to prevent anyone from hanging back. At their head, urging them on, there were often women and girls of the Communist Youth, themselves bearing arms."

One of those doomed young women was Nadya Krayevaya, who, with their comrade Sasha Bagry, picked up a rifle from a dead soldier and joined the delaying action at the cape. Nadya died in a bayonet charge; a short time later, Sasha was led off, coughing blood, in a column of prisoners.

On July 3, the last of the Russians surrendered, and the siege was officially over, 247 days after it had begun. The Germans claimed nearly 100,000 prisoners and "booty," said Manstein, "so vast that it could not be immediately calculated." The Russians had lost Sevastopol, but the propagandists who portrayed it as a heroic defeat were correct: For eight months the battle had tied down the German Eleventh Army far from the main fronts, and Manstein's last assault had taken him much longer than he had planned.

Yet by no stretch of the Soviet imagination could the fall of Sevastopol and the failure of relief efforts at Leningrad be construed as a hopeful sign for the hot days of summer, when the year's main German offensive would inevitably strike. Rather, Stalin's winter offensive and his spring campaigns had only added enormously to the long string of Red Army disasters stretching back to the Great Purge and beyond. Uncounted thousands of Soviet troops had perished so far this year, and approximately 500,000 more had been taken prisoner.

Pointed questions sprang to the minds of Soviet citizens everywhere. Sevastopol, Kerch, Kharkov—how could such horrors have happened to the Red Army? Why had so many husbands, fathers and sons perished? Was it true, as it seemed, that many of their generals had failed them? And how could the Red Army survive when the Fascist legions struck again, as they surely would in the summer?

The citizens did not know the answers to these questions. But they did know that the answers would not change anything. They were doing all they could to equip their fighting men, and they would continue to do so in the name of their righteous patriotic war.

In June 1942 the German Eleventh Army surrounding
Sevastopol was poised to take the Black Sea port and end
a siege that had already dragged on for 30
weeks. Its commander, General Erich von Manstein, had to
hurry. His troops were urgently needed elsewhere; yet
he could not risk the terrible toll of losses that would
weaken his army for the battles that lay ahead. So Manstein
made plans to obliterate Sevastopol's three rings of tough
defenses with a monster artillery bombardment, and had
received additional artillery units to reinforce his own. As
military history records, "no siege time on the German side can
remotely offer such three more formidably massed."

On June 2 Manstein gave the starting signal to his 208
batteries — 2,000 guns. In all the ring of guns erupted with
a rattling crescendo a roar. The Luftwaffe joined in with
round-the-clock bombing raids of several hundred planes.
What Manstein called the "bizarre spectacle" was, to a
beleaguered townsfolk, literally, a "whirlwind of fire." In
Sevastopol not a single shell is fired on night and
day, the whole town was in a... sounded at the start of
each bombardment, recalled the mayor, "from
then on the alert, and we never sounded the all clear."

But the city's defenders were braced for the onslaught.
Crouched in forts, in pillboxes, and trenches were 106,000
Red Army troops, some of Black Sea marines and a horde
of civilian boys and girls from the Communist Union of Youth.

Manstein's army fought on steadily for five days
and nights. By the time German infantry moved in, they "had
taken the brunt of the defense," one admiral recalled. "The
attackers ... and ... them with a storm of deadly
fire." It was late ... almost a month later, before the last
of the defenders were overcome. But then, to Manstein's
... his divisions had been so badly mauled that
for a time they were unable to go into combat again for
some ... Their capture of Sevastopol's last
mighty stronghold would inspire them throughout
the rest of the war ...

A TERRIBLE CRESCENDO TO SIGNAL THE END

And the destruction of Maxim Gorky and every other Soviet stronghold, the advancing Germans came up against the innermost line of defense of Sevastopol, a warren of hundreds of individual pillboxes, bunkers and other fortified positions, many of which were guarded with barbed wire and land mines.

The intensity of the German artillery barrage reached a terrible crescendo as the infantry prepared to move forward. Manstein was determined to flatten every last

shell exploded [...] and only after [...] long duration [...] Germans, most [...] ginkers, the Soviet [...] end on the Chersonese [...] many Russians held out [...] lost cause. There, the last [...] of resistance. Sevastopol, which [...] as the strongest fortress city in the world, finally fell to Manstein's Eleventh [...]

LIFELINE IN THE ARCTIC

An Allied convoy, nearing Murmansk in the Russian Arctic, loses a supply-laden freighter in a towering explosion after a torpedo attack by a Luftwaffe plane.

AN ICE-FREE HAVEN FOR ALLIED CONVOYS

Soon after Allied convoys began running supplies to the Soviet Union in August of 1941, the small port of Murmansk above the Arctic Circle became one of the most valuable pieces of real estate in the entire Soviet Union. Thanks to a quirk in the course of the warm Gulf Stream, the harbor at Murmansk on the Barents Sea remained ice-free even in the depths of winter, when the more southerly Soviet ports at Archangel and at Vladivostok on the Pacific coast were frozen fast. From Murmansk a rail line ran south 850 miles to Moscow, where the war matériel was distributed to the far-flung sectors of the Russian front.

The defense of Murmansk required constant vigilance on the part of Soviet troops who patrolled the treeless tundra that lay between the port and German forces in occupied Finland and Norway. In the spring of 1942, when reconnaissance patrols warned that the Germans were mounting a major offensive, the Red Army lost no time in attacking the enemy bridgehead at the Litsa River near the Finnish border. In three days of bitter fighting, Soviet units won about eight miles of terrain at the northern end of the German line. Although they were dislodged two weeks later, the Russians had succeeded in crushing German hopes of taking Murmansk overland.

Thereafter, the frustrated Germans relied chiefly on air and sea attacks to neutralize the port. In the summer of 1942, the occasional Luftwaffe raids over the city increased to four every 24 hours, and a pack of 40 U-boats prowled the shipping lanes to Murmansk.

The task of shepherding the supply convoys was shared by the British Royal Navy and the Soviet North Fleet. British warships screened the convoys to protect against U-boat attack on the first leg of the 2,000-mile journey from Scotland, and Soviet destroyers joined the escort just beyond Bear Island, off the tip of Norway. The joint force then escorted the convoys through what seamen aboard the merchant ships called Bomb Alley. In spite of heavy losses, the convoys managed to bring in more than one million tons of war matériel in 1942.

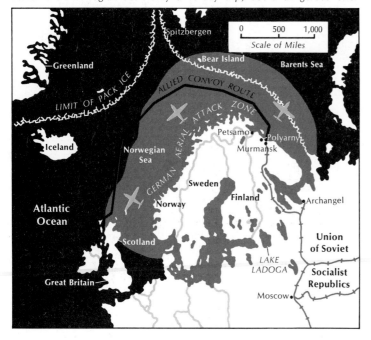

The last leg of the Allied convoy route to Murmansk led from Scotland across the Norwegian Sea—only a 10-day trip, but a dangerous one.

Carrying a heavy crate of supplies, a Murmansk civilian trudges past a bleak forest of stone chimneys—all that was left of blocks of wooden houses blitzed by cruel Luftwaffe incendiary raids in June 1942. The supply porters were, in the words of a visiting British Naval officer, "black ghosts moving in twilight over the snow in a deadly silence broken only by tinny music broadcast at regular intervals by the state."

THE CRACK SHOTS HUNTING BIG AND LITTLE GAME

The gunners who guarded the Murmansk front put in long, uneventful duty hours punctuated by brief flurries of violent action in which they excelled.

Antiaircraft artillery crews defending the port against low-level Luftwaffe raids had no hope of bagging a bomber unless they were at their weapons when the planes slipped into sight over the arc of hills that framed the city. Seconds after the bombers appeared, the pilots would unload their bombs, gun their engines and make good their escape. Yet the crews of crack shots at Murmansk claimed to have downed as many as four planes a day.

Their comrades who manned the Soviet coast artillery north of the harbor, on the Sredny peninsula, had longer waits for bigger game. Their long-range guns interdicted Petsamo, a German-held port that exported nickel essential to the manufacture of steel for the metal-starved Reich. By July 1942, the gunners were taking such a toll of German shipping that Petsamo was all but eliminated as a viable supply point.

Meanwhile, at close range on the tundra outside Murmansk, the Red Army artillerymen who guarded the rail line that led south from the port proved uncannily accurate. Once, their marksmanship saved a Soviet captain who was caught at a forward artillery observation post surrounded by a company of Germans. The captain coolly telephoned his battery to open fire on his position. The gunners complied and managed to drop their shells all around the observation post but not quite on it. When the smoke cleared, most of the Germans were dead. The Soviet artillery captain was wounded but still alive.

Proudly showing off a hunting trophy, Red Army gunners operating on the Sredny peninsula hold up a ring buoy that floated ashore after they had sunk a German transport.

Soviet sailors investigate an abandoned German Junkers-88 bomber that was beached on the shore of the Barents Sea after being crippled by antiaircraft fire near Murmansk.

Suited up in winter camouflage, Soviet ski troops load their gear and supplies into dog sleds for a sweep through the wilderness surrounding Murmansk.

INVISIBLE FIGHTERS RISING FROM THE TUNDRA

Inland from Murmansk, where winter temperatures sometimes fell to −50° F., Soviet patrols probed constantly to harass the two divisions of German mountain troops operating near the border with Finland.

"Our soldiers live in dugouts and tents," a Soviet journalist informed his readers. "They are invisible unless you come close to them. Only the bitter smoke from the iron stoves and the snowy paths of telephone wire remind you that here it is possible to not only live but fight."

Fight they did—whenever German units ventured from their own dugouts. So effective were the outpost guards and border patrols that at the end of the winter of 1941-1942 the Soviet commanders at Murmansk could boast that theirs was the only segment of the Russian front that had not lost ground to the Germans.

Leaving a dugout under an outcrop of tundra rock, a patrol sets out to reconnoiter German positions.

Silhouetted against the midnight sun, Soviet soldiers search for signs of German seaborne raiders on a rocky neck of land near the Barents Sea.

Rifle in hand, a Soviet Marine stands watch on a Navy launch patrolling the approaches to Murmansk.

Unencumbered by customary battle gear, a group of Soviet Marines outside Murmansk simulates a rousing bayonet charge for a propaganda photographer.

Readying a Soviet light bomber for takeoff near Murmansk, crewmen transfer a bomb that was carted across the snowy airfield on a reindeer-drawn sleigh.

TAKING THE BATTLE TO THE ENEMY

The Red Army forces stationed at Murmansk were augmented by some 12,000 stripe-shirted Marines and by a small but feisty air force. Though the Marines and the airmen were primarily on defensive duty, both groups earned a reputation for going after the enemy.

During the Germans' offensive in the spring of 1942, the Marines made an amphibious attack on the enemy's rear. No one is sure how many Germans were killed in the fighting, but the total was sufficient to earn the Soviet Marines a vivid sobriquet—the "Striped Death."

The Soviet Air Force detachment at Murmansk made itself feared by downing no fewer than 132 Nazi planes in a three-month period early in the War. One of the fighter pilots became legendary in the Soviet press. On a lone sortie, he met three Luftwaffe planes, shot down two, rammed the third and then bailed out. All three opponents parachuted to safety and were waiting for him on the ground. The Russian killed one assailant, eluded the other two and trekked through the snow for six days, reaching his base unscathed except for a frostbitten foot.

From an ice-coated deck, the captain of a Soviet submarine guides his ship into her moorings.

Captain Nikolai Lunin scans the sea through his periscope. By February 1942, he had sunk seven ships.

NAVAL GUARDIANS OF THE JAGGED COAST

The Soviet North Fleet, based at Polyarny, just up the coast from Murmansk, was given three missions: to protect incoming convoys, to guard the shore against German landing parties and to destroy transports sent to resupply Wehrmacht troops in Norway and in north Finland.

The destroyer squadrons that escorted the convoys into port were the most conspicuous of the naval guardians. But the invisible and unheralded force of 20-odd North Fleet subs won their full share of laurels. Wrote one Soviet submariner with a flair for poetry: "Like hunters tracking game in a forest, we furrowed the ocean in search of an enemy."

It was a brutally difficult job. In winter, the patrolling subs were sheathed in ice as soon as they surfaced, and the frozen spray made the deck gun inoperable. In the bitter cold, torpedoes would freeze in their tubes or run erratically when launched.

Yet in spite of the elements, the submariners did considerable damage to German shipping. On one occasion newspapers in the Reich protested the "inhuman" tactics of a Soviet sub that had sunk a ship carrying 30,000 sheepskin coats to the ill-clad soldiers in Norway. The Soviet captain who fired the lethal torpedo wasted no sympathy on the invaders, replying: "Let them dance in the frost. They came uninvited."

Narrowly escaping the blast of a Luftwaffe bomb, a Soviet destroyer escorting an Allied convoy keeps to her course in the choppy waters off Murmansk.

A dockside crane hoists a crate containing prized machine tools at Murmansk. The weightiest loads—tanks and trucks—were transferred ashore by crane ships that had been lent to the Soviet Union by Great Britain.

Shouldering supply crates, civilians in Murmansk help to load a freight train for the journey south. On Saturdays and holidays, when women and young people from the town joined the regular loading crews, as many as 3,500 workers swarmed around the docks.

A PAY-OFF OF DESPERATELY NEEDED WAR MATERIEL

When the Allied convoys reached Murmansk, the war matériel was hauled onto Moscow-bound freight cars by permanent crews of longshoremen. They were bolstered by political prisoners and common criminals, plus women volunteers and Russian troops who got high wages for spending their leaves working in the far north.

The labor was grinding, especially for the convicts, who were driven like draft animals and fed barely enough to keep them alive. If the convicts collapsed or were hurt, they were shot by guards.

Overall, the Murmansk operation could not supply more than about 3 per cent of the enormous Soviet appetite for war matériel. But it was a vital help, and by 1942, Soviet troops on remote fronts were growing accustomed to the goods sent from their Allies across the seas: British Spitfires, Canadian wheat and, from the Americans, jeeps, tanks and Spam.

2

Like ancient Gaul, the Soviet home front was divided in three parts. One part differed little from the battle zone and in fact coincided with it: Millions of citizens from besieged Leningrad southward to Moscow and fallen Sevastopol had dug city defenses and fought the Germans with old rifles, shovels, clubs and rocks. The second part was the immense Soviet interior, stretching eastward from Moscow 5,000 miles into Siberia. Its citizens were the shock troops of a great industrial and agricultural war to support the Red Army in the field. The third part of the home front was now enemy-held territory, where millions of Russians slaved for the Germans at gunpoint or fought the Germans as partisans. In spite of its divisions, in spite of its distances and the cultural diversity of its 16 republics, the home front in the winter of 1941-1942 was for the most part an enormous garrison manned by half-starved, half-frozen, wholly resolute people.

The Russians bore their sufferings with a stoicism that was second nature. They had endured centuries of czarist tyranny. In the two decades just past, they had endured Communist measures harsher than those imposed by other nations even in wartime: stiff travel restrictions, state censorship of all news, forced labor camps. Now to their natural stoicism was added a fierce passion. The Russians hated the German invaders with a grim fury and supported the war effort with a mystical love of country—a love that their poets described endlessly but that could be defined only as Russian.

Soviet patriotism had been raised to fever pitch on November 6, 1941, as German armies drove to within 40 miles of Moscow. That night, in a searing speech delivered in Moscow's cavernous Mayakovsky subway station, Josef Stalin called upon the people for even greater sacrifices in the name of "the Great Russian Nation," an emotion-laden phrase that the Communists had discarded as a czarist aberration in the aftermath of the Revolution. Stalin artfully orchestrated love of country and hatred for the Germans, the Russians' ancestral enemies. He damned the Nazis for calling the Slavs subhuman "Untermensch," worthy only of conquest and enslavement.

"And it is these people without honor or conscience," Stalin said with deadly calm, "these people with the morality of animals, who have the effrontery to call for the extermination of the Great Russian Nation—the nation of

HOLDING THE HOME FRONT

Plekhanov and Lenin, of Belinsky and Chernyshevsky, of Pushkin and Tolstoy, of Gorky and Chekhov, of Glinka and Tchaikovsky."

Stalin's invocation of the glorious past—of Holy Mother Russia as well as the new Soviet state—tapped the wellsprings of his people's national and ethnic pride. "The Russian people felt the deep *insult* of the German invasion," reported the Russian-born British journalist Alexander Werth, who spent the War years covering the Soviet Union. "It was something more deeply insulting than anything they had known before." The struggle against the invader took on the character of a holy war. "All for the front" became a devout slogan. Even the motto under the *Pravda* masthead was changed—from "Workers of the world, unite" to "Death to the German invaders."

The Soviet government spared no expense in its efforts to fan the flames of patriotism. The war news was carefully policed: Information took second place to inspiration, and accounts from the battle front were skillfully doctored to make the most of successes and to soften the blow of defeats. But readers soon learned how to read between the lines of *Pravda* and other newspapers. Stories that told of "fierce fighting" indicated that there were possibilities for victory. But a "complex" situation was really a grave situation, and if the phrase "heavy fighting" appeared—as it did toward the end of the siege of Sevastopol—it meant that the situation was hopeless.

For all its deceptions, Soviet propaganda was publicly accepted as an integral and idealized part of the war effort. No one complained when correspondents and war photographers, sent to the front to glorify the troops, were fed even when soldiers went hungry, and the newsmen were assigned bodyguards to protect them from capture. The heroes of the press had their own theme song, a flowery tribute composed by novelist-poet Konstantin Simonov: "With Leica and notebook, and with machine gun, we have passed through fire and ice."

The propagandists aimed ideological campaigns at several segments of Soviet society, among them members of the harassed Russian Orthodox Church. Shortly after the German invasion, the government suspended publication of blatantly atheistic newspapers, disbanded the five-million-member Society of the Militant Godless and appealed to Orthodox Catholics by vilifying the Germans for their persecution of Roman Catholics. The new policy helped—in spite of the obnoxious implication that churchgoers needed special inducements to behave patriotically. Sergius, Metropolitan of Moscow and Kolomna, praised the state for its recent enlightened attitude toward the Church and preached, "All into the ranks! Shame on all those who remain indifferent to this call!" Church donations to the Red Army followed. An entire tank column was paid for with Church funds and then blessed by a priest, whose prayer made mention of Stalin, "our common father."

The newspapers were full of editorial exhortations, which became a full-fledged patriotic art form. Perhaps the most fervent practitioner was Ilya Ehrenburg, a sometime novelist whose hate-the-German harangues were often splashed across the front page of *Red Star*, the Army newspaper. "Let us kill," he wrote in a widely quoted editorial. "There is nothing jollier than German corpses."

Russian plays also inveighed against the Germans and extolled Soviet patriotism; theater groups propagandized in the big cities and traveling troupes carried the message into the hinterlands. The message was painfully clear in Mikhail Sholokhov's *School of Hate*, which portrayed in excruciating detail the courage of a Russian prisoner of war under German torture. In a popular production by the Moscow Art Theater, Konstantin Simonov's *Russian People* dramatized the derring-do of a small band of Russians fighting the Germans in a seaside city much like Sevastopol. The third act of the play ended with the phrase, "See how the Russian people are going to their death," show-stopping words that usually produced weeping among the audience. Of course, the drama ended on a happy note—with the Red Army retaking the town. So strong was the emotional appeal of Simonov's play that it was reprinted, word for word, in *Pravda*.

By 1942, the Soviet film industry was also turning out propaganda full blast. Besides the usual boy-meets-tractor dramas, the film makers made grandiose historical epics and hard-hitting frontline documentaries, such as *Moscow Strikes Back*, *Siege of Leningrad* and, notably, *One Day of War*, which cost the lives of 30 of the 160 cameramen on the job. The most imaginative of the historical epics, *Ivan the Terrible*, was part of a campaign to equate Stalin with

Russia's towering culture heroes, who were officially described as the dictator's "Great Ancestors." It was no easy task to redeem a Great Ancestor as repugnant as Ivan, a murdering tyrant who once killed his own son in a fit of rage. But the Ministry of Cinema recruited just the man to pull it off: the renowned director Sergei Eisenstein.

Eisenstein, who affected the American show-business jargon he had picked up during a stay in Hollywood, made a valiant effort to explain to *Time* correspondent Richard Lauterbach the official reasons for Ivan's rehabilitation from cruel despot to Soviet hero. "He has been misunderstood," Eisenstein asserted. "Until late in life he was a very progressive influence. He had a farsighted foreign policy. Of course, there was an underlying pathology in his character throughout, but it didn't assert itself until his last years. In the beginning he was quite normal, see?"

Nevertheless, despite all the exhortations, despite all the burning patriotism, the task confronting the Soviet home front in 1942 was very nearly impossible. The German armies had seized about two thirds of the nation's industrial facilities and 42 per cent of its cultivated lands. For the Soviet Union to survive, vast new farmlands would have to be cleared and planted and great new factory complexes would have to be built—all this in a race against the swift striking power of the German panzer armies.

Still, the nation had formidable assets: a huge population (reckoned at 194.1 million in 1940) and enormous natural resources in a land so immense as to be virtually unconquerable. Although the Soviet government warned the people not to count on it, they might also get important help from their British and American allies, who had promised to open a second front in Western Europe and who were shipping small but increasing quantities of war matériel through the Arctic ports of Murmansk and Archangel.

The Soviet government had instituted a Draconian program of nationwide mobilization. The Army claimed the overwhelming majority of Russian men between the ages of 16 and 40; farm and factory functioned very largely on woman power, assisted by the underaged and the overaged of both sexes. Production of consumer goods—everything from floor lamps to matches—was ruthlessly curtailed. Even tractor production, essential for the Soviet collective farms, gave way to tank production, with the inevitable worsening of acute food shortages.

The government's boldest and most important wartime edict called for the mass evacuation of Soviet industry. Some 1,500 factories that had escaped the German onslaught were ordered to pack up and move thousands of miles eastward, out of reach of both German panzers and Luftwaffe bombers. This stupendous undertaking was comparable to moving all the industries of Pittsburgh and Detroit to California, and it was supposed to be accomplished in six months, over a railroad system that included only four transcontinental tracks running east and west.

To lose as little production time as possible, many factories earmarked for movement were kept in operation until the last moment. The great steel mills and the power plant in Zaporozhye on the east bank of the Dnieper River were still being dismantled and loaded onto freight cars as German forces occupied the west bank. Here, as in many threatened factories, explosive charges were set to sabotage any remaining machinery in case the Germans broke through the city defenses. The Russians tried to leave nothing behind that the enemy could use; they destroyed underground cables and even plugged up plumbing. Nothing was too big to move—not massive drill presses nor giant smelting ovens nor whole assembly lines.

Between June and October of 1941, nearly 300 major industrial complexes were evacuated from the Ukraine, along with 136 smaller factories. Close to 500 industries moved out of the Moscow area and nearly a hundred more left Leningrad just before the city was surrounded in September 1941. By Christmas 1941, more than 1,300 large plants manufacturing tanks, planes, artillery and ammunition had been shipped eastward; some 200 of them were sent to the Volga River region; about 500 went to the Urals and the remainder were moved all the way to Central Asia and Siberia. Something like 1.5 million railroad-car loads were required to complete the job.

With the plants went the workers, 210,000 of them from the Moscow area alone. All the way up and down the threatened front, factory hands packed up their belongings and followed their lathes and presses. Their destinations were the burgeoning Ural cities of Magnitogorsk, Chelyabinsk and Sverdlovsk, and the mushrooming Siberian towns of Omsk and Tomsk, and Tashkent and Alma-Ata in Central Asia, as close to Peking as to Moscow.

For almost a year, the entire Soviet Union was in a turmoil of movement. Millions of workers and refugees were shifting convulsively eastward with industry. They were joined by tens of thousands of wounded soldiers en route to rear-area cities. At the same time, millions of soldiers were moving westward. Many of them came from the Soviet Far East, where they had been guarding the Soviet Union's Outer Mongolian border against the Japanese; Japan's commitment to a Pacific war against the United States had freed them to join the battle against the Germans.

For all the eastbound workers, the transcontinental journey was a nightmare. Since most passenger trains had been consigned to military traffic, the civilians traveled on freight cars, with as many as 50 people crammed into a boxcar too small to accommodate half that number comfortably. Even at best the facilities were primitive: perhaps a wood-burning stove in a corner of the car and a hole chopped in the floor for a latrine. At way stations, meager rations were doled out. The trip was interminable; the eastbound trains were frequently shunted aside in favor of trains bound for the front. Workers might have to endure these miserable conditions for several weeks before reaching a destination in Siberia, thousands of miles from their starting point.

In winter, the journey killed. Many of the cars lacked

At an improvised print shop close to the front, Soviet typesetters select type for an edition of a Red Army newspaper. In the summer of 1942, the Army publications played an important propaganda role in helping to stiffen the Russian soldiers' will to fight; the papers appealed to the men's personal sense of honor and self-respect by printing letters from their families at home agonizing over the Red Army's long string of defeats.

stoves, and passengers by the uncounted thousands froze to death or were crippled by frostbite. Even a stove was a mixed blessing; often it was not vented and travelers choked on the acrid wood smoke. "It was crowded and stuffy and we simply couldn't breathe," recalled a worker. "Some of the men climbed up on the roof. It was freezing but we had to breathe. At night it was so crowded people took turns sleeping, often atop one another."

The travelers had to shift for themselves during long layovers, and the railroad station at Novosibirsk east of the Urals was often jammed with people heading still farther east. The huge waiting room, said journalist Lauterbach, "recalled old movie scenes of refugees at Ellis Island. Dense masses of people were sprawled on the benches, overflowing onto the stone floor. Families were sleeping on mattresses, or rolled up in ragged blankets. Around them were strewn their earthly possessions."

Lauterbach was shocked by the sight of wounded soldiers packed into their own waiting room. Here were scores of "legless, armless men en route to rest homes, sanitariums, rehabilitation clinics and farms. I had never seen so many broken men gathered together in one place before. It was an incredible picture, full of the immense suffering, patience and courage of the Russian people."

Not all of the travel scenes were grim ones. The soldiers, marking time while their trains were stalled in a station, often pulled aboard women who were waiting for a civilian train. The famed novelist Alexander Solzhenitsyn, who was a young Army officer at the time, later recalled such a scene. "The only shy one of the girls," he wrote, "sat by the stove like a little ruffled owl. In the heat, the other girls had long since thrown off their overcoats and quilted jackets and even their blouses. One girl, wearing only her red shift and flushed all over, was washing shirts for the lads."

At night the soldiers and women would share a meager meal and sing songs around the stove. "Later," Solzhenitsyn wrote, "they would crawl into the hard bunks, made of unplaned wood, to sleep, huddled together." Some of the women "would lie down and make love to the boys in the shadows away from the lamp. Why not be good to a soldier going to the front line? These days might be his last."

The end of the workers' journey east was usually a raw frontier town or sometimes a desolate wilderness site. In several places, transplanted factories went into production even before buildings had been erected around the machinery. In the southern town of Tashkent, near the border with Afghanistan, a steel plant was set up in the open, and its first furnaces and quenching baths operated around the clock in rain or snow. In some towns, canvas was stretched over machines to afford the workers a little protection until they built roofs and walls.

The new towns were singularly cheerless places. To correspondent Lauterbach, Magnitogorsk was utterly dismal. Located just beyond the Urals, it sprawled across a barren steppe toward a 27-square-mile open-pit iron mine in the distant hills. "There just didn't seem to be any city at all in the accepted physical sense of the word," Lauterbach wrote. "There were a lot of rutted dirt streets, along which were set down a series of dull, jerry-built stucco and wooden houses. Everything needed paint." Magnitogorsk had no business district, no theaters and few amenities. The center of the city was its reason for being: vast, grimy steel mills, with six huge blast furnaces, 20 open-hearth furnaces and satellite factories that turned the steel into artillery shells, heavy machinery and a dozen other finished products. The steel mills alone employed 45,000 people.

Close to half of the steelworkers were women and teenage girls. Peering through the murk of a Magnitogorsk mill, Lauterbach at first thought the male workers looked "like black dwarfs"; they were, he discovered, mostly boys, aged

Proud crew members of a Russian supply train take a break in front of their locomotive, splendidly emblazoned with the mottoes "Victory will be ours" and "Forward for the Motherland." Railroading was among the most hazardous of civilian occupations, for the Luftwaffe paid particular attention to the Soviet transportation system, mounting scores of raids each day. In just two months' time in 1942, railroaders and engineering troops repaired about 1,900 miles of damaged track— often under bombing and strafing attacks.

14 to 16 and undersized from inadequate wartime diets.

The Magnitogorsk workers, organized into "youth front brigades," labored in filthy, hazardous conditions. The mills were littered with debris; there was simply no time to waste on cleanup. Ventilation was poor and safety precautions nonexistent. Yet the workers ignored the perils and hardships. Working 10-, 12- and even 14-hour shifts, they often outstripped their government-set production quotas.

Sverdlovsk, another industrial center, was not quite so grim, partly because it was an established city and partly because it was located in an unusually handsome part of the Urals, full of lakes and woods and grazing cattle. Amid that verdant setting sat Sverdlovsk's giant industrial complex, called Uralmash. But here the factories were no less crude than those slapped together in south-central Asia. "Rain poured through the roof of the steel mill," Lauterbach reported, forming "deep pools of water on the uneven dirt floors." At the start of the War, Sverdlovsk had a population of 500,000. Transplanted war industries and their workers soon doubled the size of the city.

Omsk, 500 miles east of Sverdlovsk, was the site of a tractor works that had been shipped 1,300 miles from Stalingrad and converted to turning out T-34 tanks. The only relief from the bleak toil were occasional evening concerts and dances. At one dance, Lauterbach was amused to discover that the pretty girls were the same "grimy-faced kids" he had seen slaving away in the tank factory earlier. "I would have bet," he wrote, "that nothing so feminine and fragile had been in that factory." Most of the workers came from Leningrad, Kharkov, Rostov, Kiev, Odessa, Sevastopol—all cities threatened or occupied by the Germans. To Lauterbach's questions, they said they were resigned to making Omsk their home, during the War and after, "if that is what the government decrees."

Novosibirsk, the Chicago of Siberia, was an enormous conglomeration of wooden shacks, barracks, dugouts, tents and lean-tos that had been built in 75 days in the winter of 1941-1942, when 300,000 transplanted workers arrived on the forested steppe. Somehow the newcomers had survived, and somehow they had been organized into an efficient work force that produced munitions, military radios and field glasses, and 25 Yak fighter planes a day. "They learn very fast, wonderfully fast," said one official, adding that "a courageous worker in the Yak plant gets as much publicity as a courageous soldier at the front."

It was not so bad, wrote one girl to her mother in Moscow. Her home was a dugout, scarcely bigger than a foxhole. But "there are no bombs and after all brother Yasha had to live in a trench at the front. I have made wonderful new friends. There's the wonderful spirit of all of us sacrificing together."

The young working mothers left a deep impression on Yury Paton, an engineer at the tank plants in Chelyabinsk. "They came to the factories, often with their growing sons, performed the hardest jobs—jobs usually done by men—then stood for hours in queues for food and looked after their children, for whom they were both mother and father at once, and did not break down when the death notices arrived bearing the names of their husbands, sons or brothers. They were really heroic."

American journalist Edgar Snow asked a woman munitions worker who labored at a dizzying clip on the production line how she could stand such concentrated work. "I can go on making shells at this rate," she replied, "as long as Hitler can take them. My husband is at the front. Every time I finish a shell it brings him that much nearer home." She was speaking of war's end, not of leaves or furloughs; the distances in the Soviet Union were so great that few soldiers made trips home, even if their units granted them passes.

All told, about 20 million Russians went east—the greatest and fastest mass migration in history. They worked wonders of construction: in eight wartime months in Magnitogorsk, for example, they built a blast furnace larger than one that had taken 30 months to complete before the invasion. And together with the workers who remained at plants safely located in the west, they accomplished miracles of production.

Between the German conquests and the uprooting of industry, war production of all kinds had dropped sharply in 1941. But it began picking up again early in 1942, and then it soared. By the end of the year, tank production exceeded 2,000 units a month, which was more than eight times the previous high rate in 1940. The Soviet State Defense Committee had set a goal of 22,000 combat aircraft for 1942; by the end of that year, planes were being turned out at a rate of 30,000 a year—and the numbers were still climbing.

As might be expected, the mass migration created a huge food crisis in the Urals and beyond. In some areas, twice as many people had to live for nearly a year on local crops and a food distribution system that had been barely adequate before the German invasion. The winter of 1941-1942 and the months following were a time of privation throughout the vast interior. But things began looking up when the weather broke and new crops could be planted.

Simple but effective stopgap measures were adopted to relieve the local food shortages and cut down the need for imports from other parts of the country. The number of private vegetable gardens soared; just about everyone planted squash, potatoes, beans and cabbage, providing a substantial part of home needs. The local authorities also turned over to each factory a large tract of empty land, and somehow the workers found time to plant and cultivate crops there as well. In turn, the people's increasing self-sufficiency made it easier for the government to concentrate on supplying the Army, the cities and the infertile areas with the crops produced on the big collective farms. Each farm worker on the collectives also had his own quarter acre on which he could grow crops or raise livestock for personal use or for sale on the open market.

Many new collective farms were opened in the interior, often close to the burgeoning industrial cities. At Magnitogorsk, for example, a new collective cleared and cultivated 50,000 acres, more than half of it planted to potatoes; and on their private plots the farmers managed to raise not only mixed crops but also 14,000 cows, goats and pigs. In the southwestern Soviet republic of Uzbekistan cotton had been a minor crop before the War; now production rose so steeply that the Uzbeks were soon supplying more than 60 per cent of the country's cotton. In Samarkand, where the summer heat sometimes reached 130° F. in the shade, hundreds of thousands of new irrigated acres produced wheat, dried fruits and breeding stock for new cattle herds.

Yet in spite of dramatic progress, the Soviet agricultural program was unable to produce foodstuffs fast enough to make up for the millions of acres overrun by the Germans. At one point during the War, Stalin said that the problems of farm production were more difficult than defeating the Germans. As it was, the government had been forced to give the collectives lower priority than both the Red Army and Soviet war industry, and the farmers were left to muddle through pretty much on their own.

Wartime life on collectives everywhere was an unrelenting struggle to meet crop quotas with an inadequate supply of labor and equipment. Besides stopping the manufacture of farm machinery, the government confiscated many of the collectives' tractors and diverted them to military use; the tractors left behind frequently lay idle because fuel or replacement parts were unavailable. To make matters worse, the Soviet Union had lost 37 per cent of its draft animals, and for lack of horses and oxen, many milk cows and farm workers—including women—were hitched to the plow. Most of the harvesting was done manually, with old and young swarming through the fields with sickles, scythes, pitchforks and shovels.

Not surprisingly, large pockets of people lived at near-starvation levels through the winter of 1942-1943, and there was a great deal of grumbling about the collectives' performance, especially since some farmers got rich on the sale of crops and livestock they raised on their own plots and sold on the open market. These farmers were soon made the butt of a bitter joke. One of them, the story went, was seen carrying a big basket and a small one, and on being asked what they contained, he said, "The little one is for my vegetables and the large one for my money."

Whatever problems the Russians were facing in the interior, they were nothing compared to those besetting the people under German occupation. In the great rich regions overrun by the Germans, one third of the Soviet population suffered deprivations and brutalities unimagined by their countrymen safely behind the long battle front. The German invaders claimed that they had come as liberators, to free the Russians from the yoke of Bolshevik tyranny, and some citizens—especially those in the fiercely separatist Ukraine —had listened hopefully at first. But people of every ethnic background were quickly alienated by Nazi orders for the ruthless exploitation of the land and its *Untermensch* population. Most of the food produced in the occupied territories was shipped to Germany. "The feeding of the civilian population," said a German overseer, "is a matter of utter indifference." More than four million Russians were also sent to Germany, where they toiled as slaves and all too often perished in the enemy's factories.

In the cities and towns, many of which were heavily damaged in the fighting, the people were governed by a combination of pitiless German officers and corrupt collaborators who did little for the sick and wounded, the homeless and the orphans. With many factories crippled, unemployment ran high despite German efforts to convert consumer industries to war production. By the winter of 1941-1942, starvation was commonplace in Kiev, Kharkov, Smolensk and other occupied cities, driving hordes of im-

poverished urban refugees into the hinterlands to barter, forage or beg for food. Prices soared for whatever foodstuffs were left after the Germans had taken the lion's share.

Conditions in the countryside were only a little better. In a fitful effort to appeal to the many farmers who opposed the collective system, the German authorities broke up some collectives and distributed the land even though the Communist system suited their colonial ambitions better than private ownership. No one was satisfied with the results, not even the newly landed farmers. Freed from the disciplines of their comrades, they refused to sell their

Corralled behind a wire fence, Belorussian civilians await transport to Germany as slave laborers in 1942. All told, something like 380,000 citizens of Belorussia were packed like cattle into freight cars and shipped west, where the young women were consigned to brothels and the rest toiled 18 hours a day in the Third Reich's munitions factories.

produce to the urban centers for paper money of dubious value, and the shrinking food supply in the towns drove still more people into the countryside in spite of German roadblocks set up to stop them.

Before long, desperate civilians began heading into the hills and forests, joining with Red Army men left behind and forming small bands of partisans to combat the Germans. At the first sign of guerrilla activity, the Germans cracked down hard, putting suspects to death without anything remotely resembling legal evidence. In one such case, a widow living in a village 110 miles south of Moscow lost her grown son Kolya to six soldiers billeted in her house. The troops, four Germans and two Finnish volunteers, accused Kolya of partisan activity—puncturing a tire on a Wehrmacht vehicle—and swiftly acted on their charge.

"The moment they took him away," the widow told journalist Alexander Werth after Soviet forces had recaptured the village, "one of the Finns, with a leer, said they were going to hang him. I pushed him aside, trying to run after my son, but he knocked me down and pushed me into that small storeroom and locked the door. Later a German came and unlocked the door and said: 'Your Kolya's kaput.'" Kolya and an unknown drifter were left hanging outside the house day after day. "I could not go near them," recalled the widow, "but I could see them from the window swaying in the wind. Only three days later did the Commandant allow the bodies to be taken down. They were brought into this room, and laid down, right there. I untied their stiff creaking arms, and, as they began to thaw, I wiped the sweat and dirt off their poor faces. And so we buried them."

Inevitably, violence escalated. More and more civilians turned guerrilla, and the Germans executed more and more citizens—partisans, suspected partisans, people suspected of aiding the partisans and even whole villages near the scene of partisan activity. In a pattern familiar in many German-occupied countries, the guerrillas polarized the civilian population. Most people supported the partisans as their only hope, but many turned against them for bringing down terrible German reprisals.

The partisans led a precarious catch-as-catch-can existence. Even with clandestine aid from neighboring villages, medical supplies, proper clothing and food were scarce, and German patrols were forever scouring the countryside in search of the troublemakers. The groups had nothing to offer but the chance to fight the enemy, and it was a privilege they shared with great caution, for fear of taking in spies or weaklings.

Patriotism and hatred for the Germans were only basic prerequisites for a successful guerrilla. Some military training was essential as well, and many partisan groups co-

76

alesced around former soldiers—men who could teach the raw recruits simple tactics and how to handle the various guns they picked up in hit-and-run raids.

P. K. Ignatov, who helped organize a partisan band in the Kuban area in the northern Caucasus, looked for volunteers who could survive in the hills. "We shall live like Robinson Crusoe," he told applicants. "We shall get no orders for supplies or repairs up there, no shops will be open for us, no postman will bring us the latest newspapers. But we don't want, like Robinson Crusoe, to clothe ourselves in animal skins and live in shacks. Each of our partisans must know several civilian skills."

Ignatov collected a cadre of men who had mastered valuable crafts unrelated to their normal civilian jobs. "Pavel Pavlovich Nadryag, an oil engineer, turns out to be a first-rate farrier and harness maker," Ignatov later wrote. "Nikolai Demyanovich Prichina is an ardent amateur radio operator. Yakov Ilyich Bibikov, the director of our margarine plant, seems to be quite a fair cobbler, and even Mikhail Denissovich, the director of the oil-extracting plant, is a skillful ox driver."

Ignatov's group and uncounted others grew steadily more proficient and aggressive. By the summer of 1942, their raids, ambuscades and sabotage were more than a mere nuisance to the Germans. In recognition, the Soviet government proclaimed them "soldiers of the Red Army in the rear of the enemy" and exhorted them to make conditions "unbearable for the enemy and all his accomplices." Many bands had acquired machine guns, mortars and radios; a few groups even captured field artillery and antitank guns.

The best-organized bands undertook ambitious military operations. Ignatov's partisans boldly planted mines in the road to Novo-Dmitriyevskaya Stanitsa south of Rostov, then deployed in a wood full of twittering birds to wait for one of the German convoys that often took this route. "The long hours passed very slowly," said Ignatov in a melodramatic report on the action. "Suddenly a strange note was heard amid the twittering. Perhaps the distant patter of horses' hoofs? No, it was the rumble of an engine, far, far away.

"Gripping their grenades tightly in their hands, the men waited motionless in the roadside bushes. The clang of tanks treads and the rattle of heavy machine guns were now distinctly heard. Evidently the Germans feared the presence of partisans and as an extra precaution they were sweeping the bushes."

The guerrillas let the lead tank pass, and also the following trucks loaded with German troops. Then, in the usual position, came the partisans' target—the trucks bearing supplies and ammunition.

The signal to attack was an explosion—the lead tank

Three orphaned children weep beside the ruins of their home after German troops swept through their village in the Caucasus Mountains in 1942. According to the Soviet government, the Wehrmacht ravaged more than 1,700 towns and 70,000 villages in its invasion of the U.S.S.R.

Escaping from the Germans, a collective-farm woman carries her child through a marsh toward Red Army lines north of Moscow in October 1942. During the first year of the War, hundreds of thousands of Russians fled eastward, intensifying local shortages of food, lodging and medical care.

MUDDLING THROUGH A LIFE OF SHORTAGES

Muscovites queue up at a kiosk for the daily edition of Pravda. Citizens were avid not only for news of the War but for the paper it was printed on.

The rigors of war taxed the fortitude and ingenuity of Soviet citizenry all across the land—and nowhere more so than in great cities such as Moscow. The Muscovites were forced to contend not only with subsistence-level food rationing, but also with desperate shortages of virtually everything else. How they made do was a triumph of the human spirit.

Oil and coal for heating and cooking were among the scarcest commodities. Outside Moscow, 100,000 or more wood-cutters harvested fuel for the city. The timber brigades included Muscovites of every age and profession. Not even ballerinas were exempt. One night in 1942, just before the start of the ballet *Don Quixote*, the audience learned that the prima ballerina could not perform; she had recently returned from gathering wood, and her muscles were too stiff.

Timber barges brought the wood to the city, where it was then loaded onto trucks or trains and distributed throughout Moscow. Mountains of wood were piled in city squares, where people could draw their rations.

Clothes were so hard to come by that men's shoes sold for as much as 6,000 rubles, six months' wages for a factory hand. Citizens who had never touched a needle or a cobbler's knife learned to remake old clothes and patch up shoes with scraps of leather until they fell to pieces. "It's not uncommon," wrote an American correspondent, "to see a Russian seated on a curb trying to repair a shoe well enough to see him home."

The shortage of tobacco led the citizens of Moscow to dry and smoke oak leaves and aromatic herbs. And the lucky owner of a real cigarette took on the status of an entrepreneur—standing on a street corner and charging passersby two rubles for a puff.

During the darkest days of the War, even tea was hard to come by. Ina Rubin, a precocious 12-year-old, later recalled that "instead of tea we used pumpkin peel, cut up in small pieces and dried." Ina also remembered how "we made our own matches, from glycerin and manganese dioxide bought from a pharmacy. But soon the chemicals ran out and after that we used flint."

Nothing was wasted. Muscovites saved their empty bottles, boxes and string and used them again and again; such things were simply not manufactured for civilian consumption in wartime; and when supplies ran out, there was no more. Indeed, a newspaper, once so easily discarded, came to have a veritable catalogue of uses. "First they cut small pieces from it for cigarette papers," wrote Walter Graebner in *Life*, "then they use it for wrapping and finally they take it to the bathroom or place it between the blankets for warmth."

An elderly man gathers firewood, chopped by a corps of drafted civilians.

A resourceful smoker uses the sun and his glasses to light a cigarette.

Moscow's streetcars, pressed into service to replace trucks commandeered by the Army, haul sacks of cement for fortifications to the outskirts of the city.

blowing up on a mine. The long line of partisans charged into the road, heaving grenades and Molotov cocktails at the nearest vehicles. "Fire bottles were flying, grenades bursting, and the machine guns rattled without interruption. Heavy trucks dashed down the road, crushing the wounded under their wheels in a desperate effort to find a way out of this fiery circle. But there was no way out.

"Suddenly a new sound was heard amidst the din of battle. A Fascist tank, riding in the rear of the column, dashed into the bushes, to the rear of the partisans. In an instant it would have crushed this handful of men. But Genya rushed out to meet the tank.

"A Fascist spotted him and fired a short machine-gun burst at him, but the bullets flew wide. Unhurriedly, as if at his exercises, Genya swung his arm, hurled an antitank grenade and swiftly dodged behind a tree. The tank halted and abruptly stopped firing."

Then came a loud, repeated whistle—the signal to retreat. "A second Fascist column had arrived and the Germans were trying to surround the partisans. But the covering party went into action. Grenades were heard bursting in the woods while our riflemen held up the German submachine gunners. In the same instant the main attacking group leaped out of the fiery ring.

"The partisans proceeded in single file along the wild-boar tracks, forded rivers, climbed the mountains, descended into deep gorges, crossed the winding, capricious mountain rivers and at last arrived at the camp."

As indicated by the sudden appearance of the second German column, the Occupation forces had quickly developed effective measures for countering guerrilla attacks. The partisans' records, which tended to embroider on successes and minimize failures, admitted serious reverses. "In January 1942 our work began to meet difficulties," reported a partisan coordinator behind German lines in the Leningrad area. "The partisan units departed to Kholm to fight there. Through informers the Germans came to know of the existence of partisan units. They succeeded in killing Comrades Vinogradov, Shuyev, Gegorov, Vorobyov and some other activists. The work of activists was very difficult, since they had to be prepared to be captured at any moment by the Germans."

Another leader confessed that his band had lost 20 men killed and 14 men wounded, but hastened to add that in the same period it had taken in 32 new recruits. He was just breaking even: The unit consisted of 66 men and had suffered nearly 50 per cent casualties.

It was typical of the partisans that they could find some victory in the midst of disastrous defeat. After a bloody week of German reprisals southwest of Leningrad, during which 30 villages were burned down and 150 civilians were tortured and shot, the local leader wrote, "The success of our propaganda was made evident this week. The population did not betray the partisans or tell of its connection with them." As the partisans saw it, each man they lost was a hero gained. One report related how "Comrade Osipov was captured and bestially tortured by the Germans. His eyes were cut out, a hot wire was pulled through his nose—but, being a proud Russian, an honest son of the Party, he did not reveal anything to the German beasts."

Between their unquenchable optimism and their real successes, the partisan groups in 1942 laid the groundwork for major gains in the future. The groups located near the battle front established radio contact with the nearest Red Army headquarters and learned how to coordinate their operations with local Soviet counterattacks. Just as important were their political activities, which were frequently guided by party directives. Partisan leaders worked closely with the committees heading collective farms, drawing many recruits from the ranks of farmers. They even managed to reestablish collectivism on some of the farms that the Germans had parceled out to private enterprisers. In time, their political activities would combine with their growing military strength to create "partisan regions"—large areas behind enemy lines that had been restored to Soviet government even before the Red Army returned.

The bulwarks of the home front—the great cities in or near the battle zone—were now only ghosts of their former selves. By January of 1942, the population of Moscow had been reduced at least 50 per cent by the draft, the eastward movement of industry and the flight of residents who feared that the cities would come under German attack when the weather broke. Moscow had also lost a number of its government bureaus and foreign embassies, which had been evacuated several hundred miles east to Kuibyshev and other cities on the upper Volga. The War had deprived all the western cities of food, fuel and light.

On a trip to Moscow, journalist Werth heard grim stories of "unheated houses, with temperatures just above or even below the freezing point, with water pipes burst and lavatories out of action; in these houses one slept smothered—if one had them—under two overcoats and three or more blankets." The stories, Werth discovered, were all too true. With the loss of the nearby Moscow coal fields, which had supplied most of the fuel for the capital, life had become a struggle simply to keep from freezing to death. In many apartment buildings, there was no heat at all, and the residents either moved in with luckier relatives or clustered about small wood stoves with flue pipes sticking out the nearest window.

The fuel shortage hit hard at Moscow's power plants and left the city dolefully dark after sunset at 2 or 3 o'clock on the winter afternoons. Electrical power was strictly rationed. "Notices were distributed to every home," wrote American correspondent Henry Cassidy, "limiting use of electricity to a single bulb for each room, taking not more than 16 watts for a living room of up to 15 cubic meters, 25 watts for kitchens and 16 watts for washrooms and toilets." The fine for a violation of these rules was 1,000 rubles, a month's salary for the average industrial worker. Furthermore, electric hot plates could be used only four hours each day—and electric heaters were forbidden.

The city dwellers lived on a subsistence diet. Bread was the main ingredient of every meal and sometimes the only ingredient; the standard ration for workers was a bit more than one pound a day. Workers were supposed to receive five and a half pounds of meat each month—the equivalent of one very thin lamb chop every other night. But lamb and beef were seldom available, and the "meat" ration usually

Renowned composer Dmitry Shostakovich wields a hose during a fire drill on the roof of the Leningrad Conservatory of Music as the Germans attack the city in July 1941. Between blazes, Shostakovich composed his monumental Seventh Symphony in tribute to the beleaguered citizens of Leningrad. At right, with the city still under siege in 1942, a young soldier purchases tickets from a street vendor for a performance of the great work to be held in Leningrad's Philharmonic Hall.

consisted of sausage—or dried salted fish. Workers were also to receive a monthly ration of about two pounds of fats—butter or bacon—but these were usually in short supply. Nonworking dependents—older people and children —received a much smaller ration of all items; their diet amounted to a few slices of bread a day and a pound and a half of meat a month. The chronic shortage of fruit and fresh vegetables caused widespread scurvy.

The people spent hours each day waiting in line outside the cooperatives to buy whatever edibles were available. "People brought along stools and chairs with them," recalled Soviet staff officer Ivan Krylov, "and women sat there knitting and darning socks." Krylov saw a shoemaker who brought his equipment along and mended shoes while waiting in line. And most of the food was of poor quality. "The bread was black, soggy and underbaked," Krylov said. "When it was one day old it was hard as a brick. The flour of which it was baked was eked out with sawdust." Even bad bread was sometimes unavailable. With grim humor housewives called their string shopping sacks "perhaps bags."

Such idle witticisms did not escape the notice of the secret police. NKVD agents in plain clothes often queued up in food lines to eavesdrop on shoppers for a "public morale bulletin," which they regularly submitted to their much-feared chief, Lavrenty Beria. Ivan Krylov, who accidentally got a glimpse of one such bulletin, discovered that many people had highly unorthodox opinions; some were quoted as saying that after the War the NKVD would be abolished. Unaccountably, the NKVD did not act to suppress such heresies, which normally would have earned the speakers 10 years of hard labor in Siberian penal camps.

In spite of all the shortages, luxuries were available—at a price. Soviet citizens could obtain small quantities of tea, butter, sugar and vegetables in what amounted to a state-run black market. Early in the War, the Soviet government had set up a chain of food outlets—quite separate from the regular cooperatives selling rationed food—where farmers could market for profit the extra produce they grew on their own small private plots. The farmers were allowed to charge whatever the traffic would bear: for example, a pound of butter—the product of a private cow grazed in a private plot—cost 500 rubles, about half of an industrial worker's wages for a month. Still, the workers had money left over after paying their low government-regulated rents and buying cheap rationed foodstuffs, and some of them were always willing to splurge.

For all their shortages, the Muscovites managed to maintain a simulacrum of normal life. Shopkeepers opened for business daily with poor and meager consumer goods to offer; merchants acted as clearinghouses for secondhand items, earning commission money for selling people's old razors, unwanted bronze busts and surplus clothing. Industrial workers bound for the few remaining factories waited patiently in line to board the subway, and in the evenings they queued up for tickets to Moscow's circus or the ballet.

Leningraders admire the abundant harvest from a cabbage patch in front of St. Isaac's Cathedral, one of the city's great landmarks. To ease the awful food shortage created by the endless siege, the citizens tended gardens on every bit of open soil, even between the antiaircraft guns in the parks.

Children played their games in the streets, including a wartime version of hide-and-seek called partisans. But always there was tension in the air—a sense of watchful, fearful waiting. People crowded around the newspaper kiosks when the next edition was due. In all of the cities from Moscow to Omsk, citizens anxiously followed the heartbreaking stories of a city whose sufferings beggared their own: blockaded Leningrad.

The siege of Leningrad dragged on and on. More than three million citizens had been cut off by the surging German armies in August of 1941, and ever since then the city and the Soviet troops defending it had refused to surrender in spite of bombing raids, incessant artillery shelling, heavy snows, temperatures as low as 61° below zero and mass starvation. By December the city's plight was desperate. Leningrad was then struggling along without fuel, running water or electric lights. The survivors had consumed all their pets and were subsisting on a tiny ration—a few mouthfuls of bread a day.

January of 1942 was the blackest month for Leningrad. Countless citizens fell dead in the snow-covered streets, and children dragged sleds bearing the dead to the burial grounds. The Germans continued to close in, driving to within three miles of the city on its southern perimeter. Luftwaffe planes dropped millions of leaflets urging the Leningraders to save themselves by accepting the status of an open city. The city council called a meeting and composed Leningrad's answer: "Death will be afraid of us before we are afraid of death."

By February, Russians everywhere were on tenterhooks, waiting for the imminent completion of a bold relief project that the newspapers gave the thrilling name Road of Life. In the past autumn, as soon as Lake Ladoga had frozen over, Red Army engineers on the eastern shore had begun driving wooden piles through the ice into the lake bed. The piles supported a narrow causeway that was strong enough to bear the weight of supply-laden trucks. And as the Road of Life neared the city, 50 miles across the lake, a substantial stockpile of food was building up on the Soviet shore, where a new railroad branch line terminated. The whole Soviet Union had rallied to send Leningrad help. Gifts of food came from Siberia and Central Asia and even from Sevastopol, then caught in a life-or-death struggle of

its own against the Germans. Partisan groups, learning belatedly of Leningrad's suffering, had raided German depots and smuggled food through the enemy lines to the east coast of the lake.

The Road of Life was finally completed on February 10, and the trickle of supplies that had begun crossing the lake rose to a steady stream. Toiling early and late, the truck drivers brought Leningrad tons of flour, sugar, American canned meats, medical supplies, gasoline and ammunition. By the end of the winter they had delivered 360,000 tons of supplies, and the famine slowly began to relax its grip. Conditions were further improved by the start of mass evacuation, first on the trucks' return trips and then by boat when the lake ice broke up. Ultimately, about 900,000 Leningraders would be sent to safer places in the east.

By April, the worst was over, and the home front breathed a transcontinental sigh of relief. No one knew how many Leningraders had died of all causes by then; guesses ran from a half million to a million and more, and an Extraordinary State Commission finally placed at exactly 641,803 the number of citizens who had died of starvation during the blockade. And hundreds of thousands of citizens were barely alive. At the end of March, when the Leningrad city council ordered everyone who could walk to clean up the wreckage and look for unburied dead, less than a quarter of a million emaciated people were strong enough to turn out.

And the dying continued. The Germans still commanded the land approaches to Leningrad, and their artillery shelled every corner of the city at will. On occasion, when German armies elsewhere met with defeat, the gunners before Leningrad took revenge on the city with especially heavy bombardments. More buildings were destroyed, and few were left without shrapnel scars, which the Leningraders called "German kisses." Death would remain the normal way of life in Leningrad until January of 1944, when the Germans were finally driven beyond artillery range.

Russians everywhere continued to read and to worry about Leningrad, and its citizens' heroism fortified them for the terrible fighting yet to come. More than courageous Sevastopol, more than valiant Moscow in the autumn of 1941, Leningrad was the paradigm of home-front defiance, stamina and sacrifice. And so Leningrad would remain until it was overshadowed by the "Hero City" of Stalingrad.

·[.] PEOPLE TOT·[.]LLY AT WAR

Red Army crews gratefully accept a line of tanks—each proudly labeled Moscow Farmer—from farm workers who pooled their savings to pay for the weapons.

"IT WAS OUR COUNTRY WE WERE DEFENDING"

"All for the front! All for victory!" was the ringing Soviet slogan, and citizens lived it to the letter.

Children gathered medicinal herbs and scrap metal: In a single day, an official Soviet history reported, the youth of a Moscow district collected enough metal for 14,000 heavy artillery shells. When necessary, factory workers labored around the clock, while farmers slaved to exceed their quotas of crops and meat and milk and cheese. Soldiers went off to war with bouquets of flowers from the women-folk, and a patriotic female, young or old, offered her seat on the bus, train or trolley to a man on leave.

It was a time of stringent rationing, yet civilians sent food packages—as well as millions of sheepskin coats, felt boots and wool socks—to the troops. "We were poor," recalled a worker who donated some clothes, "but to the front—we gave what we had."

The Red Army never lacked manpower, yet civilians of all ages and both sexes continually sought to volunteer. When one graybeard was refused because of his age, he protested, "If I'm too old to fight, I can drive a truck. I'll go with the soldiers, I'll help up ahead and they'll follow on foot." Like the old man, Ivan Boiko and his wife, Aleksandra, were determined to go to the front. But Ivan was a truck driver and Aleksandra a factory secretary, and they were told that they were too valuable to be released from their jobs. Undaunted, the couple saved enough money to donate a tank, then got permission from Stalin to enroll in tank school and upon graduation drive their tank into battle.

The spontaneous contributions of the Boikos and others made wonderful propaganda, and the Kremlin was continually exhorting the population to greater and greater effort. But the people really did not need to be rallied, for as one scientist put it: "The best time of our lives was the War because at that time we all felt closer to our government than at any other time in our lives. It was not *they* who wanted this or that to be done, but *we* who wanted to do it. It was not *their* war, but *our* war. It was *our* country we were defending, *our* war effort."

At a blood-collection center, nurses pack blood from donors before shipping it to the front. Such centers handled as many as 200 donors a day.

Supporting the Red Army in both word and deed, a Russian family (top) writes a letter full of love and encouragement to one of their relatives at the front, while citizens in the Far Eastern town of Khabarovsk (bottom) sort the scrap metal that they collected for munitions factories.

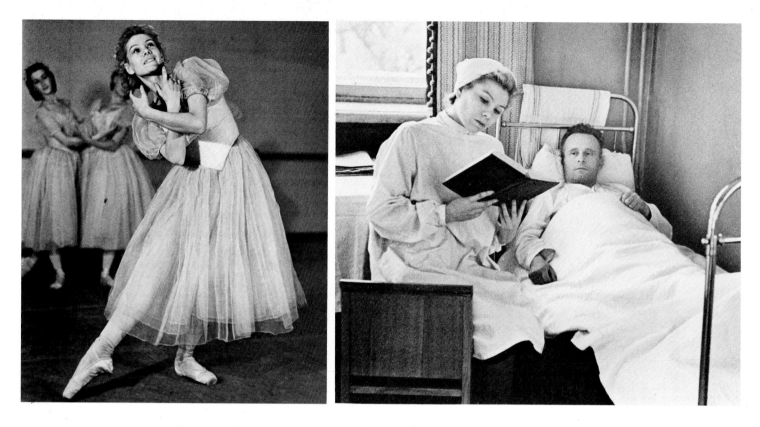

FORGING A WEAPON OF SOVIET ARTS

From the very first days of the invasion, Russian singers, musicians, dancers, actors and writers threw themselves headlong into the war effort. "We constantly felt that our Soviet art was a weapon," one actor said, "a sharp weapon like a sword. It lives, glows and warms the heart."

The artists gave performances at training bases, garrisons, rest areas and hospitals. One indefatigable singer set a record of sorts by visiting 60 wards in a single day. And the performers were no strangers to the front. Red Army and civilian theater brigades were always touring battle zones; there were nearly 1,000 such brigades, and in a single year they staged 150,000 shows.

The frontline entertainers put on their shows wherever possible—in trenches, on trucks, in tents or in birch groves. Sometimes they were under enemy bombardment. The director of one troupe remembered putting on a show in a barn where "loud applause drowned the rattle of enemy mortar shells exploding nearby. Twice we saw our audience off to battle and met them a few hours later."

Usually, the performers at the front had only a curtain for scenery and a few basic, easily transported instruments such as violins, banjos, guitars or accordions. Nevertheless, the shows were full of life and variety. During a typical performance for infantrymen on the Stalingrad front, a theatrical brigade from Moscow sang a ballad about the Cossacks, read Russian poetry and prose, staged comedy routines and performed a Hungarian folk dance.

Another troupe, which called itself the Happy Raiders, specialized in sharp-edged sketches about German Propaganda Minister Joseph Goebbels and Anglo-American promises of a second front—the second-front sketch was particularly pointed. It featured an Englishman who kept assuring the Russians that the Allies were going to invade Europe. But by the end of the skit, he had grown a flowing white beard and was still making promises.

Ballerina Marianne Bogulubskaya dances for officers at Moscow's Bolshoi Theater and reads to a wounded soldier in a nearby hospital.

A touring theater brigade uses a tank for its stage as it performs before a large crowd of appreciative soldiers in the Ukraine.

A caravan, bearing a sign proclaiming "Bread for the Front," heads toward a government collection point. These farmers were donating precious sacks of

grain *from their own share of the harvest.*

Farmers pack gifts of tobacco, butter, honey, apples, eggs and wheat flour for shipment to the front.

SOWING THE SEEDS OF VICTORY

Throughout the War the Soviet Union suffered from an acute food shortage. The Germans had conquered the Ukraine, the nation's breadbasket; the military forces had drafted virtually all the able-bodied young men from the farms; and the Army had commandeered uncounted thousands of tractors and farm horses to pull artillery and supply wagons. Yet the nation had to be fed, and the remaining farmers—women, children and oldsters—responded magnificently to the task.

On one collective north of the Caucasus, an aged farmer was assigned to mow half a hectare of grain per day; using nothing but a hand-held sickle he reaped almost three quarters of a hectare, and explained, "I have four sons in the Red Army and I want to help them as much as I can."

The farmers on the collectives frequently gave food that was rightfully theirs. By law, a collective was required to turn over 65 per cent of the harvest; many farms proudly set aside "defense hectares" just for the war effort. In addition, individual farmers freely donated food from their private plots—food that would have brought high prices on the open market.

The farmers, of course, found it was impossible to fill all the wartime food needs. But they did keep the nation alive, and they guaranteed that the Red Army was more or less adequately fed.

An official (left) accepts piles of rubles collected by farmers to buy guns.

BUILDING AN ARSENAL WITH CITIZENS' SAVINGS

On the 9th of December, 1942, the Communist newspaper *Pravda* published an unusual exchange of letters. The first letter, addressed to Josef Stalin, told how the collective farmers of Tambov Province south of Moscow had donated 40 million rubles to build tanks. Stalin's reply read, "Convey to the collective farmers of Tambov Province my fraternal greetings and the gratitude of the Red Army."

As *Pravda* had undoubtedly hoped, that was the start of a great outpouring of gifts from citizens all across the land. For weeks afterward, almost half of *Pravda* was filled with telegrams and letters from donors. "I have decided to donate all my savings toward the construction of a plane," wrote one generous patriot. "The Soviet regime made me a rich collective farmer. Now in these terrible days, each of us must help our Motherland."

By the end of the War, the Soviet citizenry had contributed some 10 billion rubles (the equivalent of 800 million wartime U.S. dollars) to build a formidable arsenal of tanks, planes, artillery, armored trains, torpedo boats and submarines.

A patriotic family, Ilya Shirmanov, his son Andrei and his wife, Maria, sits

surrounded by Andrei's comrades upon the tank bearing the inscription "Gift to our son" that Ilya and Maria purchased for their country with their savings.

THE RISING FLOOD OF ARMS

Awaiting repairs, a Soviet tank hangs from a crane in a Moscow factory. Workers in 1942 repaired hundreds of old tanks and doubled their output of new ones.

GENUINE SOLDIERS AT THE FACTORY LATHES

As late as the spring of 1942, the Allies doubted that the Soviet Union would be able to manufacture arms quickly enough to repel the German invaders; the enemy had captured or destroyed immense quantities of Red Army war matériel and nearly two thirds of Soviet industry. Yet by the end of 1942, Russian workers, using what remained, had outstripped Germany's production. In this Herculean effort, the Russians that year reportedly produced 24,700 tanks, 25,400 planes and 33,100 guns of 75mm and over, while German factories turned out only 9,300 tanks, 14,700 planes and 12,000 guns of 75mm and over.

The Soviet Union accomplished this astounding feat by mobilizing every resource. Hundreds of factories were dismantled and moved bodily far to the east, out of the Germans' reach. The production of nonmilitary goods virtually ceased: Plants that had manufactured motorcycles now made submachine guns, tractor factories were converted to tank assembly lines, and watch factories turned out fuses for artillery shells. In the emergency, corner-cutting was officially endorsed as a means of speeding production.

Industrial machines and assembly lines were manned primarily by teenagers, elderly pensioners and housewives—anyone who had not been drafted for military service. These citizens toiled 12 to 16 hours a day, six days a week—and when necessary they stayed at their machines around the clock. Many took part in a nationwide Socialist competition to raise productivity. One competitor at a Ural factory exceeded his single-shift quota by 1,480 per cent and finished his quota for five months in 15 days.

The workers knew they would receive extra pay and honors for their efforts, and that they might be punished for failing to meet their quotas. But with rare exceptions factory hands were driven by patriotism rather than incentives or intimidation. "Here in the rear, we feel that we are genuine soldiers at the front," a worker in the Urals wrote in his diary. "Sometimes it seems that the front line lies somewhere beyond the hills surrounding the city, and the explosions in the quarry—they are the salvos of our artillery."

At a Ural iron mine, a huge shovel fills a railway car bound for a steel mill. Ore from the Urals replaced that of the Ukraine, held by the Germans.

Replacements for drafted workers, a pint-sized boy—who must stand on boxes to run his machine—and a gray-bearded retiree toil in Soviet arms factories.

Female workers assemble PPSh submachine guns at a former automobile factory in Moscow. During World War II, 51 per cent of the U.S.S.R.'s industrial workers were women.

PPSh 1914G SUBMACHINE GUN

The 7.62mm PPSh boasted the highest rate of fire of any World War II submachine gun: 900 rounds per minute. The MP40, its German counterpart, fired 500 rounds per minute.

DEGTYAREV DP 1928 LIGHT MACHINE GUN

The Red Army's standard light machine gun, the 7.62mm DP 1928, was an effective weapon, despite its problems. The gun was hard to load, its thin steel magazine was easily damaged and its operating mechanism was likely to break when the gun barrel heated up.

To supply speedily the millions of small arms needed by the Red Army, the Soviet government had no choice but to sacrifice quality in nonessential parts. Ordnance experts restricted production to a relatively small number of simple, easily fabricated weapons—some of which were outdated models whose only recommendation was that they could be made quickly.

Wherever possible, stamped-steel parts were substituted for machine-tooled parts, and under hurry-up orders from Moscow, factories shipped out many guns with unfinished wooden stocks. Inevitably, some of the Soviet firearms were the crudest-looking weapons issued to a regular army during the War.

The PPSh, the Red Army's standard submachine gun, was the acme of simplicity. Many parts of the PPSh were welded together, the fastest and cheapest means of assembly. To economize on raw materials and labor, workers sometimes fashioned two barrels simply by cutting in half the lengthy barrels of old rifles, which had been warehoused in enormous quantity. Some four million PPShs were made in the course of the War.

The Soviet small-arms policy produced plenty of weapons, but of mixed quality.

The reliable PPSh submachine gun was envied by the Germans for its high rate of fire, and the Goryunov machine gun was an indestructible gem. But the Degtyarev light machine gun had a number of minor bugs, and the Simonov antitank rifle was ineffective against the thick armor of the Germans' medium and heavy tanks.

Generally, all the weapons were durable: They had few moving parts to wear out and few complex mechanisms to go wrong. They were also easy to operate and to clean—important assets in view of the fact that droves of Soviet troops were hurried into combat with little training.

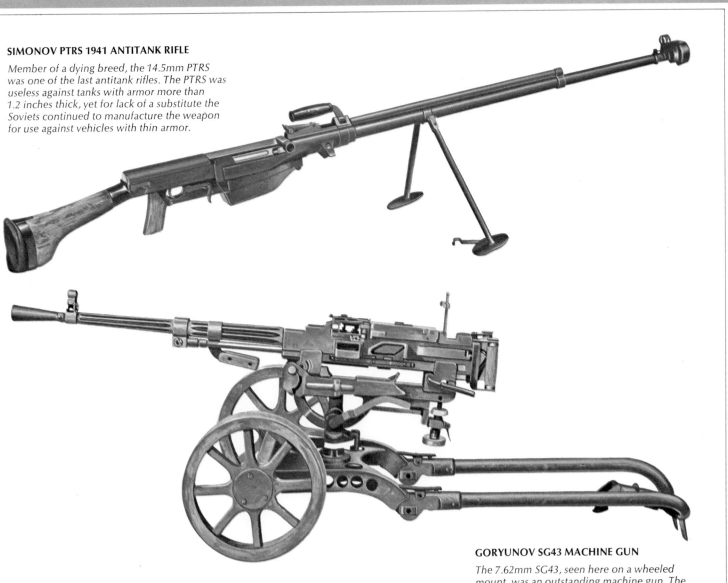

SIMONOV PTRS 1941 ANTITANK RIFLE

Member of a dying breed, the 14.5mm PTRS was one of the last antitank rifles. The PTRS was useless against tanks with armor more than 1.2 inches thick, yet for lack of a substitute the Soviets continued to manufacture the weapon for use against vehicles with thin armor.

GORYUNOV SG43 MACHINE GUN

The 7.62mm SG43, seen here on a wheeled mount, was an outstanding machine gun. The Goryunov was simple to produce, easy to operate and virtually immune to jamming.

76.2MM DIVISIONAL GUN

The work horse of Soviet artillery, the 76.2mm divisional gun served as both a field gun and an antitank gun. It could hurl a 14-pound high-explosive shell nearly 15,000 yards, and its armor-piercing shell could rip through 3.62 inches of steel from a distance of 550 yards.

ENORMOUS OFFERINGS TO STALIN'S "GOD OF WAR"

KATYUSHA ROCKET LAUNCHER

*The Katyusha, an adjustable metal framework
containing up to 16 rocket-launching tracks,
could be raised to any desired firing angle. The
weapons were frequently mounted on trucks
but they could also be set up on the ground. The
rockets had a range of about four miles.*

Josef Stalin liked to call artillery the "god
of war," and he saw to it that during the
War his ground forces had more field guns
than the German Army. The Soviet artillery
pieces were also more appropriate to the
terrain. Formidable weapons such as the

76.2mm divisional gun were light enough
to be hauled by teams of horses through
mud or snow that bogged down the heav-
ier artillery used by the Germans.

One of the Soviets' most successful artillery weapons was the simple, inexpen-

sive "Katyusha," the first effective multiple-
rocket launcher. When the Katyusha was
introduced to combat in 1941, the rockets'
screaming launches and their long trails of
flame so terrified the German invaders that
some men fled the battlefield.

"THE BEST TANK IN THE WORLD"

When the U.S.S.R. was invaded in June 1941, the Red Army had four times more tanks than the Wehrmacht, but most of them were light, obsolete or out of commission for some reason. Besides ordering an all-out maintenance drive, the government doubled and redoubled the production of modern tanks. Cutting corners as ordered, factories sent many tanks to the front roughly finished and unpainted.

Almost half of the new tanks in 1942 were 27-ton T-34s—improved versions of a model introduced in 1940. As more and more T-34s rumbled into battle, panzer pioneer Heinz Guderian conceded that it was "the best tank in the world." True, the T-34 had a cramped turret and usually lacked a radio. But none of the essentials had been neglected. The tank was faster and more maneuverable than its German opponents: Its 76.2mm cannon and two machine guns gave it more firepower, and its thick, sloped armor gave it better protection against shells. Although the T-34 was outclassed by the German Panther in 1943, the Germans were unable to produce enough Panthers to match the Soviets' output of improved T-34s.

T-34/76C MEDIUM TANK

A radical advance in engineering, the T-34 had a top speed of 32 mph and, thanks to its light diesel engine and 120-gallon fuel tank, it was able to cover 150 miles without refueling. Wide tracks kept the tank going through mud and snow that stalled German panzers.

A worker toils on a Ural T-34 assembly line. Some plants reportedly reduced the tank's production time from 110 hours to less than 40.

Factory workers consign a newly completed tank to a Soviet Army official. Sometimes, the Russians said, soldiers helped to finish a tank—and then drove it off to the front line.

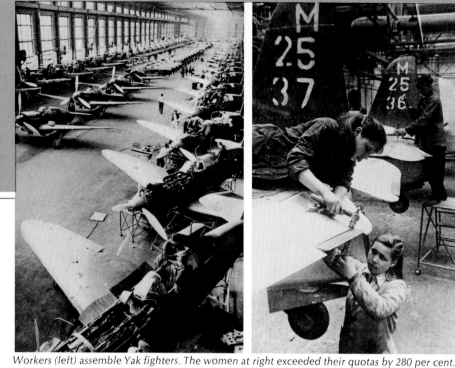

The Soviet Air Force, which was shattered by the Luftwaffe in 1941, pressed a rebuilding program that by 1942 was producing large numbers of modern fighters designed to support ground troops.

The new planes lacked the power and speed of German fighters, and because of aluminum shortages, they were constructed largely of wood. But they were exceptionally light, nimble and easy to maintain, had a maximum range of more than 500

Workers (left) assemble Yak fighters. The women at right exceeded their quotas by 280 per cent.

YAK-1M FIGHTER

Slightly lighter and smaller than the original Yak-1, the Yak-1M had a top speed of 360 mph, and at altitudes of 6,000 to 13,000 feet it was able to outmaneuver the Luftwaffe's famed Messerschmitt-109. As indicated by the red, white and blue propeller spinner and emblem on the fuselage, this particular Yak-1M was assigned to the Normandie-Niémen Regiment, a unit of Free French pilots who came to the Soviet Union to combat the Germans in 1942.

miles, and were rugged enough to operate on rough runways in the wild extremes of the Russian weather.

The most widely produced Soviet fighters were Yaks, sturdy, agile planes developed by and named for Aleksandr S. Yakovlev. Yakovlev created several improved models, such as the Yak-1M pictured below. But since all were modifications of the basic Yak-1, the factories continued production without retooling.

THE MANY VIRTUES OF THE FLYING YAK

3

By mid-June of 1942, three mighty German armies were poised in attack positions north of Kharkov, ready to launch Operation *Blau*—Hitler's great thrust toward Stalingrad and into the Caucasus farther south. These armies were the Second, the Fourth Panzer and the Sixth, which had helped to smash Marshal Semyon Timoshenko's forces in the Izyum salient just a few weeks before. The three armies, forming a force later designated Army Group B, were under the command of Field Marshal Fedor von Bock, and their attack date was set for June 28.

Two more armies, the First Panzer and the Seventeenth, were assembling far to the south of Kharkov for the offensive into the Caucasus. Their attack would start in early July, at which time they would be constituted Army Group A, under the command of Field Marshal Wilhelm von List.

The armies north of Kharkov were now straining at the leash. They had been fully resupplied after their Izyum victory, and replacements had been fed into the ranks to make up for their moderate casualties. Security was tight and marvelously successful. The troops had moved to the starting line without arousing the slightest suspicion among the Soviet units on the other side of the front.

Hitler was firmly in control and showing good form. When Timoshenko had made his dangerous Izyum breakthrough in May, the Führer had had plenty of units hidden in the rear areas, waiting to assemble for the big offensive, and a jittery commander in chief might have thrown them into a counterattack. But Hitler refused to commit any forces that might tip off *Blau,* and the divisions already engaged had bounced back to finish the job. Also to his credit, the Führer had put into effect an imaginative deception program that improved considerably *Blau's* chances for an uncomplicated success.

This program was code-named Operation *Kreml* (Kremlin), and its object was to prevent intervention in *Blau* by the huge Soviet reserve that was piled up south of the Moscow front to block any German thrust toward the capital from that direction. Hitler had no plans for a Moscow offensive, but *Kreml* simulated enough activity to keep the Russians worried. German headquarters on the Moscow front issued a top-secret directive ordering "the earliest possible resumption of the attack on Moscow," and followed it up with many phony supporting orders. Two pan-

THE MARCH OF THE MASTODONS

zer armies facing Moscow went through elaborate attack preparations, with only a few of their own officers privy to the fact that no part of the operation would ever take place. Reconnaissance flights over the Moscow area were stepped up, and German intelligence officers were instructed to ask prisoners of war questions about the Moscow defenses; the Germans knew that the Soviets routinely planted agents among surrendering soldiers and that these agents could somehow get news back to the Red Army High Command.

The Germans cleverly made it hard for the Soviets to piece together a picture of the spurious offensive—just hard enough, that is, to convince them that it was real. The Soviet commanders swallowed the red herring whole and wasted a great deal of effort bracing the Moscow defenses.

Everything was breaking right for Hitler. But suddenly, on June 19, Operation *Blau* fell into dire jeopardy. A shocking breach of Army security had taken place.

This stupidity had been committed on June 17 by no less a personage than Lieut. General Georg Stumme, the skillful and aggressive commander of the Sixth Army's 40th Panzer Corps. General Stumme, whose red face—due to high blood pressure—had earned him the nickname Fireball, had assembled his three division commanders to brief them for the first time on the corps's assignments in the first phase of Operation *Blau*. Quite correctly, Stumme had given his instructions verbally, as Hitler had expressly ordered. But one of the commanders had asked for a few notes to keep his memory fresh, and Stumme later obliged. He dictated a half-page outline, had a copy made for each division commander and arranged to have reliable couriers deliver the copies to the three division headquarters north of Kharkov.

On June 19, after receiving Stumme's illicit memorandum, Major Joachim Reichel, operations chief of the 23rd Panzer Division, made an ill-fated decision to fly to 17th Corps headquarters to check his division's deployment in *Blau*. He took with him the memorandum and his own map, marked with the placement of the 40th Panzer Corps's divisions and their objectives in the first phase of *Blau*. Reichel boarded a Fieseler Storch observation plane at 2 p.m.; he never reached his destination. The plane strayed off course, was hit by Soviet antiaircraft fire and forced down near enemy lines with a bullet hole in its fuel tank.

None of this was known to the Germans for nearly eight hours. That night at his headquarters in Kharkov, Fireball Stumme threw a lavish dinner party for his division commanders and five other important officers. Stumme was a noted gourmet and proud of it; he always said, "War's bad enough—why eat badly as well? No, gentlemen, not me!" He regaled his guests with caviar, roast venison and Crimean champagne, and he jokingly called the feast "the condemned man's last meal." But he and the officers were in high spirits and were looking forward to *Blau*.

At about 10 p.m., a sergeant interrupted the cheerful chatter to call Stumme's operations chief, a Lieut. Colonel Hesse, to the phone. As Hesse left the room, Stumme called after him jovially, "Don't come back with bad news!"

Hesse came back with a bombshell: Major Reichel's plane was long overdue. As Hesse explained that Reichel had departed with the *Blau* plans, Stumme leaped into action. He ordered his aides to telephone every division, regiment and company to ask if anyone had seen Reichel's plane.

For an hour Stumme and his guests paced, fretted and imagined the worst: The plane had been shot down behind Soviet lines and the plans had fallen into Russian hands. Finally word came through from the 336th Division. One of its forward observers had seen a little plane go down in the late afternoon; it had landed just behind or very close to the Soviet lines.

Stumme ordered a reconnaissance party to search the front at once. The scouts found the plane in a small valley in no man's land. It was intact but there were no papers in it, and all useful instruments had been removed. The German reconnaissance team found two fresh graves and assumed that the Russians had shot and buried Reichel and the pilot. Unhappy but satisfied, they returned to their lines and reported in.

Stumme was furious. "Since when," he shouted, "have the Russians shown such respect to our dead as to bury them?" Stumme feared that the Russians not only had the plans, but also had Reichel. And he guessed that they had buried two other bodies in an attempt to deceive any German investigators.

To make sure, Stumme ordered another patrol; Reichel's orderly went along to identify the major's body if it was indeed in one of those graves. The graves were opened, but the bodies had been stripped and were so badly mutilated that the orderly was not able to make a positive identification. Now Stumme's scenario for disaster was complete. He imagined that Reichel was at that very moment having his fingernails torn out by the Soviet secret police and that he was revealing everything about *Blau* that the Russians could not deduce from the telltale papers. Before long, great numbers of Soviet forces that had been pinned to Moscow by Operation *Kreml* would be moving south to Stalingrad to thwart Operation *Blau*. Or so Stumme supposed.

The fate of Reichel was to remain a mystery: The Germans never learned it, and the Russians never revealed it. But the fate of General Stumme and his leading colleagues soon became a matter of Wehrmacht record. The commander of the 23rd Panzer Division was relieved of his post three days before the start of *Blau*. Stumme and his chief of staff were court-martialed and sentenced to five years and two years of imprisonment respectively. However, the presiding officer of the court-martial, Reich Marshal Hermann Göring, sympathized with good soldier Stumme and appealed to Hitler for clemency. The Führer commuted Stumme's sentence and sent him to North Africa in time to get killed in action at El Alamein in October 1942.

As D-day for *Blau* loomed, Hitler briefly rode the horns of a dilemma. Should he scrub *Blau* on the assumption that the Russians knew all about it? Or should he go through with the offensive? Icily, Hitler made his decision: on with *Blau*.

It was the right decision, even though the Russians knew a great deal about *Blau*. Soviet troops, as the Germans surmised, had indeed found Reichel's plane, and the papers were in their hands. Since the aircraft had come down on Timoshenko's front, the papers worked their way upward through channels to the marshal himself. Timoshenko divined the importance of the plans, described them over the phone to Stalin and forwarded them for his scrutiny.

Stalin interpreted the papers in the light of his mistaken preconceptions—that the Germans intended to attack Moscow from the south and that they had planted phony papers in order to lure his Moscow defenders out of position to fight a nonexistent or secondary thrust toward Stalingrad. Belated aerial reconnaissance confirmed that German troop dispositions jibed with the plans, but no matter. Stalin simply did not believe a word about *Blau*.

Even if Stalin had believed the evidence before his eyes, there was no obvious reason to think that the Soviets could stop Operation *Blau*. The Red Army was apparently incapable of breaking its long tradition of colossal defeats, demoralization, desertion, mismanagement, miserable intelligence, poor tactics and worse strategy, and destructive meddling by political commissars and by Stalin himself. The Red Army seemed to be hopeless.

And yet certain signs of resurgence could be detected

even amid the Red Army's most appalling failures. Although Timoshenko's Izyum attack had been a disaster, it might well have succeeded had it not run head-on into German formations prepared for an offensive of their own. Just six months before Izyum, the Red Army had lacked both the daring and the experience even to contemplate such a lightning thrust. And though Stalin had insisted on the assault, he had listened to reason and eliminated several utterly foolish attacks elsewhere.

The Red Army could be rebuilt. It was, in fact, being rebuilt on the battlefield, forming a huge hard core of experienced survivors—independent-minded commanders, capable field officers at the battalion level, tough noncoms who had the confidence to function on their own initiative. In the next several months, even as the Russians fought to stem the tide of Operation *Blau* at Stalingrad, the rebuilding process would raise a Red Army significantly better in overall performance.

The basic ingredient for rebuilding was, of course, the Russian soldier—the peasant, the worker, the clerk, wrested in seemingly inexhaustible supply from the enormous Soviet population. What could be expected from a soldier who was given hasty training and sometimes treated almost as badly by his superiors as by the enemy? To the German press in the flush of the Wehrmacht's Izyum triumph, the Russian soldiers could do nothing right because they were "a mixture of low and lowest humanity." But they had what a Soviet staff officer called "the fight-to-the-death spirit," and the raw troops who survived a few months of battle became formidable soldiers with a recognizable sense of *esprit de corps*.

Troop morale was further improved by the home-front factories, which by June 1942 were supplying the Red Army with substantial quantities of serviceable weapons. Infantry units that were short on rifles six months before, now had large numbers of submachine guns. Although the Soviet soldier was one of the world's worst wastrels when it came to ammunition, he was nonetheless a fearsome figure as he sprayed the landscape with submachine-gun fire. "The men were guided by a psychological factor," explained a Soviet general. "It was easier to advance with the butt of a belching submachine gun pressed to your stomach."

In the days immediately following Timoshenko's Izyum

fiasco and the disaster on the Kerch Peninsula, the Red Army possessed barely 200 tanks south of the Moscow front. But again, salvation came from the home front—in a manner unbelievable to Hitler. Chief of the General Staff Franz Halder had warned the Führer in midwinter of intelligence estimates indicating that the Russians were producing 600 to 700 tanks a month; for his pains, Halder had been treated to the spectacle of Hitler slamming his fist on the table and declaring, "Impossible!" At that time, Halder's figures were probably exaggerated. But now, during the rebuilding period for the Red Army, Soviet tank production was in fact rising toward a rate of 2,000 each month.

These tanks represented vast improvements over early models. Even the original T-34 had caused the Germans consternation when it was well and valiantly employed. In October 1941, a force of T-34s manned by the instructors and cadets of the Kharkov tank training school had met the onrushing panzers of the Wehrmacht's famed General Heinz Guderian in a battle at Tula, south of Moscow. The Russians in their T-34s had hurled back the panzers, causing Guderian, Germany's tank warfare genius, to reflect after the War: "Up to now we had enjoyed tank superiority, but from now on the situation was reversed."

A German sergeant gave an enlisted man's view of the action. "The Russian tanks are so agile," he wrote, "at close ranges they will climb a slope or cross a piece of swamp

Soviet antitank teams assemble with their long-barreled weapons for a prebattle ceremony in which they pledge to fight to the death. The two-man rifles were not powerful enough to punch through a heavy tank's armor, but they were deadly when used to blind eye ports and periscopes.

Red Army mortarmen line up for inspection with their weapons broken down into components and strapped to their backs. Soviet artillery losses were so severe in the early stages of the War that for a time these highly mobile mortars furnished much of the Army's close-fire support.

faster than you can traverse the turret. And through the noise and vibration you keep hearing the clangor of shot against armor. When they hit one of our panzers there is so often a deep long explosion, a roar as the fuel burns, a roar too loud, thank God, to let us hear the cries of the crew."

The new T-34s coming into action in 1942 had better guns and engines. And they retained the broad tracks that made them more mobile and more weatherworthy than German vehicles. In mud or snow they could—quite literally—run rings around the panzers. The turret of the earlier T-34 had been difficult to operate, and its large hatch was vulnerable to grenades and satchel charges; the hatch had been replaced by a smaller opening for the commander and a second one for the gunner. The rear overhang of the turret—a favorite place for German tank-killer squads to plant their mines—was eliminated, and handrails were welded onto the rear deck so that infantrymen could be carried to counter enemy antitank teams.

The heavily armored KV tank, first employed on the Leningrad front in December 1941, was just now arriving at the front in appreciable numbers. Throughout its lifetime, the 47-ton KV would cause Wehrmacht forces the same consternation that a German general described on his first encounter with the behemoths. Twenty KVs "overran the rifle regiment and broke through into the artillery area. Shells from all the defensive weapons bounced off the thick enemy armor. Our 100 tanks were unable to check the 20 gigantic tanks and suffered losses."

Even after 88mm antiaircraft guns were brought up to disable a few Soviet giants and disperse most of the rest, the German combat groups spent the next two nights and days at the mercy of a single KV that rambled through their supply area, cutting the units off from food stocks and ammunition and preventing the evacuation of increasing numbers of wounded. The engineers who laid demolition charges under the tank's tracks at night reported that the standard charge had done nothing more than chip the giant's ponderous plates. On the third day, the Germans deployed 50 tanks to the front and sides of the KV and engaged it long enough for an 88mm gun to be brought into position 600 yards to its rear. Finally, after 12 direct hits, the great tank expired.

In spite of its new weaponry, the Red Army was not yet ready for sophisticated offensive maneuvers, and tactical formations, particularly infantry, were developed in recognition of that fact. The result was a rough-and-ready order of battle that made relatively modest demands on the expertise of commanders and required of the ordinary soldier only that he be disciplined and proficient in the use of his particular weapon.

The evolving rifle divisions were an outgrowth of the 5,000-man rifle brigades that had been thrown together in 1941. With 9,600 men, the divisions were almost twice the size of the brigades, and they were far more heavily armed with automatic weapons. The rifle division was also efficient in its use of manpower: Less than 6 per cent of its soldiers were engaged in rear-area support functions, as opposed to 15 per cent in a German infantry division. Moreover, the Soviets could slap together a rifle division in

A troop of Cossack cavalry charges across a shallow stream along Russia's Voronezh front in September 1942. At its peak during the War, the Red Army included more than 200,000 horsemen—who were attached to infantry divisions for patrol and reconnaissance duty, and organized into frontline cavalry divisions and corps for combat on their own.

a few weeks from local peasants fresh off the training ground or with virtually no training at all. Just as easily, a rifle division could be fought to virtual destruction before being disbanded or rebuilt. Its job was to put massed firepower on a given objective—and hang the human cost.

"If we come to a minefield," General Georgy Zhukov once explained, "we attack exactly as if it were not there." The justification for such assaults was provided by a brutal equation: "The casualties we get from personnel mines we consider only equal to those we would have gotten from machine guns and artillery if the Germans had chosen to defend the area with strong bodies of troops instead of minefields."

Nevertheless, the Soviets were learning the lessons of modern war. Tank formations were becoming more powerful and tactics more sophisticated. At the start of the War, a

Soviet tank brigade contained only 30 tanks, many of them obsolete, and was almost devoid of shielding infantry support. It was thus highly vulnerable to light, nimble German antitank teams. As it developed in 1942, the Soviet tank brigade boasted no fewer than 63 T-34s, with two full companies of infantrymen attached. It was a formidable spearhead unit, with its own infantrymen riding on the tanks and firing submachine guns in all directions to keep the enemy infantry at bay. The Soviet tank-borne troopers would dismount and reduce antitank gun positions or fortifications when they were encountered, then remount to continue the assault deep into the enemy's lines.

There was still much to learn. The debacle in the Izyum salient had provided a bitter lesson in the perils of uncoordinated mass attacks. And the Soviet tank commanders were working to master the techniques of hitting the Ger-

mans from the sides and rear. They were learning to take advantage of their vehicles' superior qualities, and they were studying ways to combine tank attacks with cavalry, infantry, artillery, engineers and close-support aircraft.

In other departments, the Red Army also had cause for optimism. It had always had a respectable proficiency with massed artillery. By the summer of 1942, the Soviet artillery commanders had rediscovered—at heavy cost—the need for employing their bigger guns in large specialized units, always located well to the rear of their protective infantry. In 1942 they were producing better cannon than the Germans, and would soon be producing more, outgunning the superior German artillerymen with sheer weight and range.

When concentrated artillery was available, the planners hewed to the dictum that a constant barrage should be laid down on enemy positions while the infantry worked its way forward into rifle range. Sometimes the artillery would continue to fire even as the infantry attacked, leaving lanes open in the barrage pattern through which the foot soldiers could make their way. When they achieved the objective, the infantry would dig in and wait for the artillery to be brought up to cover the next advance.

Similarly, Soviet combat engineers had long since gained a reputation among the Germans for effective exploitation of natural conditions and materials. Soviet commanders were giving their opponents nasty surprises in the arts of concealment. And the discipline instilled by the party and the Army paid off particularly well in the Army's unfailing ability to move men and equipment silently through the hours of darkness, to conceal their tracks and deployment during the day, and to spring upon the enemy from total darkness just before dawn.

The Russians were already masters of the difficult art of crossing rivers. When the Germans had to cross the Dnieper River, both in attack and retreat, they were able to average only one crossing per 30 miles. In similar circumstances, the Russians did 10 times as well, finding or constructing some means of getting their troops and equipment across every three miles. Their engineers were particularly adept at building floating bridges, a major feature of their training, and in addition they contrived to construct bridges that could be sunk for concealment and then raised to permit a surprise crossing. Sometimes fixed bridges were built with their treads a foot below the surface, making them invisible to German observation.

Forests and villages attracted Soviet commanders like magnets, the Germans observed, because their engineers were so good at turning them into strong points. A riverside village or a patch of woods leading to the water was sure to be used for a concealed attack approach. Trees were cut with astonishing speed to prepare hidden artillery positions; with equal rapidity, trees were turned into corduroy roads through forests and marshes. The infantry was used to cut trees, lay tracks and haul equipment over rough terrain, tramping paths through forests deep in snow when necessary. Reported one German general: "Ten men abreast, with arms interlocked and in ranks 100 men deep, prepared these lanes in 15-minute reliefs of 1,000 men each."

The Russians' retention of large units of cavalry long after the ancient arm had been abandoned by other major armies gave the planners and the Red Army greater flexibility in operations over difficult terrain, and particularly in severe weather. Horses could operate in mud, marshland, and in any sort of broken ground; they could filter through forests and negotiate watercourses and ravines that would halt motorized units.

The horses could survive at 22° below zero and keep moving in dust and sand that clogged and wore out engines. Cavalrymen could fight as infantry after covering immense distances, and like the motorized infantry, they could exploit breakthroughs punched by tanks. In attack and defense their capability for concealment and rapid dispersal could catch the enemy off guard or force him to move with caution. When operating over broad fronts, the abler Soviet commanders advanced their tanks and infantry over main roads and meadows and used the cavalry to cover the higher and more-difficult terrain in between. The Red Army's planners provided for expanding this arm, and by 1942 they were building toward 200,000 mounted cavalrymen organized into nearly 40 divisions.

The Army benefited not only from improving tactics, but also from changes in the demoralizing system of dual command between military officers and political commissars. Inevitably, the commissars undermined the authority of the field commanders, who found it virtually impossible to win and keep their men's confidence. The commissar system had been abolished in August 1940, only to be reinstated in July 1941. But now, in the early summer of 1942, the heyday of the commissars was again nearing an end.

The latest decline of the commissars began after the May 1942 disaster on the Kerch Peninsula. The botching of the Soviet defenses had been due in large part to the blunders of Deputy Defense Commissar Lev Mekhlis, later described by Nikita Khrushchev as "a nitwit" who had helped turn the People's Commissariat of Defense into "a kennel of mad dogs." Stalin had demoted Mekhlis, and thereafter, interpreters of Soviet policy were fascinated to find in *Red Star*, the Army's official publication, which slavishly echoed Stalin's views, a suggestion that commissars were meddling too much in military affairs; they were executing frightened soldiers too readily and neglecting their true role as morale builders. Not until October 1942 were the commissars officially downgraded to a position as "political deputies" to the actual combat officers. But in the meantime most of them had got the word, and they began tending more carefully to their nonmilitary duties.

When fulfilling his proper function the commissar could, especially at the lower levels of the Army, genuinely enhance the soldiers' welfare by acting as a combination of teacher, morale officer and, in a highly secular sense, chaplain. When not actually in combat, the troops spent two sessions daily under the tutelage of the commissars, listening to lectures and readings calculated to instill unquestioning loyalty and discipline and to educate them in the current Kremlin attitude toward the world outside their units and their villages.

Rote indoctrination in every aspect of the party's teachings was the objective, and several evenings a week were devoted to question-and-answer sessions in which "cor-rect" responses were rewarded with privileges and amenities. Inadequate and incorrect replies brought restrictions and on-duty study assignments in which backward soldiers were coached by their more enlightened colleagues.

The commissars were supposed to see that soldiers wrote home regularly, and they were available to write messages for the illiterate. As the Army's censors, they made sure the letters were ideologically correct. Through the political chain of command extending back to the home front, the company-level commissar did what he could to solve the soldiers' domestic problems and to ensure that the letters he received were equally pure and inspirational. The commissars arranged sports and entertainment, supervised post exchanges and published unit newspapers at every level of the Army. They were expected, moreover, to inspire their comrades with heroism in combat—and the list of commissars killed in action was a long and honorable one.

To Stalin, the diminution of commissarial power was bitter medicine, and for his country's survival as well as his own hide he would have to swallow worse yet. Clearly, the Red Army could no longer afford military commanders who owed their positions to toadyism or to their doctrinaire political beliefs. Gradually, painfully, these party functionaries were being weeded out and replaced by a new breed. Most of the new leaders were in their forties; until recently, many of them had been politically suspect, and they had proved their mettle not in labyrinthine Kremlin corridors but on the battlefield.

Among the most notable of these was the Polish-born Major General Konstantin K. Rokossovsky, a victim of the Great Purge, whose mouth, as a result of torture at the hands of Stalin's secret-police inquisitors, was equipped with twin rows of metal teeth. Like Zhukov, his colleague and commander in the defense of Moscow in the winter of

Red Army political commissars gather in February 1942 for a propaganda meeting. The military role of these Communist Party officials—whose ranks included future Soviet Premier Leonid Brezhnev (front, center) —was abolished later in the War because of the confusion created by the Army's dual system of military and political authority.

1941-1942, Rokossovsky had begun life with the Red Army as a cavalry officer in the civil war. During the early 1930s he had commanded the 7th Cavalry Division in the annual war games and had distinguished himself as a practitioner of mass breakthrough and rapid envelopment of opposing armies. The games were part of a program instituted by Marshal Mikhail Tukhachevsky, the leading proponent of a modern Red Army, and the chief martyr in the purge.

As if his growing reputation as a Tukhachevsky disciple were not enough to land him in Stalin's dungeons, Rokossovsky also ran afoul of the venomous Commissar Mekhlis, on whose orders he was arrested, beaten to insensibility and charged with selling out to the Germans and the Japanese. A civil-war comrade named Yushkevich, it was alleged, had implicated Rokossovsky in the treasonous plot. But at his trial, instead of humbly confessing to his crimes, Rokossovsky sarcastically pointed out—and the records confirmed—that Yushkevich had been killed in action in 1920. This was too much even for Stalin's servile judges; Rokossovsky was finally released and sent back to the Red Army.

Rokossovsky was undeniably a hard man to handle. He did not observe the protocol of awaiting a go-ahead from the Kremlin before making the slightest move, but instead insisted on acting on his own initiative, trusting his own judgment. In June 1941 he refused to obey Stalin's orders to ignore the German units facing him, and he also dismissed Zhukov's advice to "relax, the Boss knows best." Instead, Rokossovsky prowled his frontline positions right up to an hour before the German attack, keeping his troops on the alert and advising his subordinates and those of the adjoining corps to "stick close to your units." As a result, Rokossovsky was the only Soviet general able to mount a counterattack during the first awful month of invasion: In July, he led a mechanized shock corps against the 4th Panzer Group and held it up for a week.

In August near Smolensk, Rokossovsky handed the Germans their first defeat: Operating under Zhukov's command, he stopped an enemy column, counterattacked and drove it back in a grinding, relentless drive that recaptured Yelnya and very nearly trapped a considerable German force. Later, at Moscow, Rokossovsky's Sixteenth Army contained and helped to hurl back the last German thrust at the capital. Later, when the billboard-sized portraits of the heroes of the defense went up all over Moscow, the number

of Rokossovsky posters was exceeded only by those of the scowling Zhukov.

This, then, was just the sort of man the Red Army so urgently needed—a cool tactician, tenacious on defense, savage in his assaults, independent. Rokossovsky's example would inspire Soviet Army commanders in the battles at Stalingrad; he himself would participate in the final rout of the Germans, and later would go on to great glory in the ultimate destruction of the German war machine.

Similarly, the iron doors of an NKVD cell opened just in time to cough up the Red Army's leading artillery expert. Nikolai Nikolayevich Voronov, a clerk's son, had soared from artillery private to commander of a Red Army artillery division during the civil war. Big guns were Voronov's passion and, while attending the Frunze Military Academy in the 1930s, he vaulted into the front ranks of Soviet artillery thinkers with his highly respected thesis on "The Development of Artillery Technology and Its Influence on Strategy and Tactics in the First World War."

Early in 1941, Voronov's advocacy of increased mortar production was opposed by none other than NKVD boss Lavrenty Beria, a military ignoramus who for some reason considered himself an artillery authority. Beria resolved the dispute by clapping Voronov into solitary confinement. And it was there, deep in the bowels of prison during the initial German onslaught, that Voronov was asked by Stavka, which had nowhere better to turn, for his recommendations as to how Soviet artillery might be saved from oblivion. His memo won him not only his freedom but also appointment as inspector general of artillery, a post from which he immediately initiated reforms. One of his first acts was to order the increased mortar production that had landed him in jail. And he went on to assemble the great masses of artillery that would come into play in the Soviet counteroffensive at Stalingrad, shattering enemy lines and opening the way for encirclement of the German Sixth Army.

Among top Soviet staff officers, the humdrum voice of Aleksandr Vasilevsky was increasingly heard. He was the son of a priest and, like Stalin, had once attended a theological seminary; now, clearly on the ascendancy as Stalin's military adviser, he displayed the patience of someone long accustomed to awaiting conversion. By his every military instinct, he favored Zhukov's theory of the strategic defensive—followed, after the enemy had worn itself out, by a crushing offensive. But Vasilevsky was no man to butt against Stalin's obduracy. At the March conference that had led to Timoshenko's disastrous offensive, Vasilevsky had remained silent. Thereafter he had bided his time, tending to myriad staff details, acting as a buffer between Stalin and his field commanders, and husbanding his persuasive powers toward the day when he would help devise and bring before Stalin a brilliant plan for victory at Stalingrad.

And then, of course, there was General Georgy Zhukov. Beloved by few, feared by many, professionally respected by nearly all, he was called behind his back the Beetle (from his name root, zhuk, which means "beetle," or even "cockroach"). He was coarse, profane, bullying, brutal; yet for all his roughneck ways he was a serious military scholar, steeped in the works of the great commanders and theorists from Caesar to Clausewitz—and possessed of an extraordinary capacity for learning from experience.

For Zhukov, the experience that shaped subsequent successes had come on a remote and improbable battlefield in a little-known, undeclared war. In May of 1939, amid the bogs and marshes of the Khalkhin-Gol River area on the Mongolian-Manchurian border, sporadic clashes between Soviet and Japanese frontier troops had mushroomed into a conflict in which the Japanese attacked with an infantry division, a motorized company and substantial cavalry forces. By the end of June, nearly 36,000 Soviet and Japanese troops and more than 300 tanks were embroiled, with the Russians getting distinctly the worst of the fighting. At that point, Zhukov was assigned to the Soviet command.

Zhukov dug in, grimly adhering to the defensive while awaiting reinforcements—which, since the nearest Russian railhead was almost 400 miles distant, were agonizingly slow in coming. Yet, by mid-August, Zhukov had built up a superiority over the enemy of 1.5 to 1 in infantry, 1.7 to 1 in machine guns, almost 2 to 1 in artillery and 4 to 1 in tanks. Then and only then was he ready to take the offensive.

He took remarkable care to mask his intentions. Working parties ostentatiously continued to prepare defensive positions. Trucks without mufflers were run noisily back and forth along the line to drown the sound of tanks being moved into position. Zhukov even saw to it that a certain

115

manual fell into enemy hands. Its title: "What the Soviet Soldier Must Know in Defense."

Just as Zhukov's every action so far bore the hallmark of his later operations against the Germans, so too did his planned offensive, which envisaged breakthrough, encirclement and annihilation. As it happened, the Japanese managed to break out of Zhukov's pocket, but they were nonetheless flung back across the disputed border.

The battle of Khalkhin-Gol came to an end during the first week of September 1939. During that same week, Hitler's armies marched on Poland, and the action at Khalkhin-Gol was forgotten—by everyone except Zhukov. He not only remembered but used Khalkhin-Gol as the prototype for

the sequential strategy of defense, build-up and attack that proved so successful at Moscow. He had argued for that same strategy before Izyum and had received a stinging rebuke from Stalin. But now, in the wake of Timoshenko's debacle, the dictator was beginning to listen to his foremost field commander.

And none too soon—since powerful German armies were poised for the massive offensive with which Hitler intended to end the war on the Russian front.

On June 28, two of the three armies led by Field Marshal von Bock exploded out of the Kursk area 90 miles north of Kharkov. The Fourth Panzer Army, followed by the Second

Churchill and Stalin crack wan smiles for photographers during their grim conference.

A CHILLY MEETING OF UNFRIENDLY ALLIES

On the 12th of August, 1942, Prime Minister Winston Churchill—unrelentingly anti-Communist since 1917—flew to Moscow to tell his old adversary Stalin that there would be no second front in Europe in 1942. Bearing bad news to the beleaguered Russians, said Churchill, was like "carrying a large lump of ice to the North Pole."

Stalin listened glumly to Churchill's explanation: The Allies lacked enough landing craft and U.S. troops for an assault on the heavily fortified French coast. Stalin perked up a bit when Churchill sketched a crocodile and explained how an attack on North Africa scheduled for November would open the way for an assault on the "soft underbelly" of Hitler's Europe.

In their next meeting, Stalin returned to the issue of a second front in France. He accused the Allies of fearing the Germans. The Prime Minister retorted, "I pardon that remark only on account of the bravery of the Russian troops," and commenced what American representative Averell Harriman termed "one of the most brilliant statements I ever heard from Churchill." The interpreter was unable to keep up, and Stalin finally stopped the speech with a smile, saying, "Your words are of no importance. What is important is your spirit."

Over dinner the next night, as the mood mellowed, Churchill asked Stalin if he had forgiven him for opposing the Bolshevik Revolution after World War I. "All that is in the past," Stalin replied. "It is not for me to forgive. It is for God to forgive."

Army to the north, roared straight east toward Voronezh, about 100 miles away. The town, on the Don River at its junction with the smaller Voronezh River, was at the center of all north-south Russian rail, road and river communications between Moscow and the Black and Caspian Seas.

Two days later Bock's third massive attack group, Lieut. General Friedrich Paulus' Sixth Army, kicked off from Kharkov and slashed northeast toward Voronezh. This army was unusually strong, possessing 11 divisions and a panzer corps—the same crack 40th Panzer Corps that General Fireball Stumme formerly commanded. With the 40th Panzer Corps driving ahead to clear the way, the Sixth Army was supposed to hook up with the northern force, trapping the Soviet armies between the Oskol and Don Rivers. That done, the entire German offensive assemblage would wheel down the Don, execute another pincers, seal off Stalingrad and surge into the Caucasus.

The plan looked perfect on paper. And during the first few days, it seemed to be working equally well in practice. By June 30, panzers of the northern force had raced halfway to Voronezh in the celebrated "Mot Pulk" formation—a motorized square, with moving columns of trucks and artillery framed by a protective screen of tanks. German propagandists called the "Mot Pulk" the "Irresistible Mastodon," and one inspired hack proclaimed it "the formation of the Roman Legions, now brought up to date in the 20th Century to tame the Mongol-Slav horde."

The Sixth Army met virtually no resistance, and the troops were a little uneasy about this. One of Paulus' panzer divisions, recently arrived from Paris and now wearing an Eiffel Tower insignia, received a greeting calculated to increase its edginess. "Men of the 23rd Panzer Division," said an air-dropped Soviet leaflet, "we welcome you to the Soviet Union. The gay Parisian life is now over. Your comrades will have told you what things are like here, but you will soon find out for yourselves." The peculiar lack of enemy opposition disturbed a discerning German war correspondent accompanying the advance. "The Russians," he wrote, "who up to this time had fought stubbornly over each kilometer withdrew without firing a shot. It was quite disquieting to plunge into this vast area without finding a trace of the enemy."

The strange Soviet withdrawal that had so bemused the

Germans was by no means uncalculated. The commander of the Soviet front, the same Timoshenko who had failed at Izyum, had been ordered by Stalin—probably on Zhukov's advice—to fall back in an orderly fashion in the direction of Stalingrad. There the Red Army would make its stand—and if all went well, the Germans would batter themselves into exhaustion against the Volga bastion.

At the moment, however, Stalingrad was anything but a stronghold. Time was desperately needed to prepare its defenses and to delay the enemy advance. Timoshenko and other Soviet commanders were instructed to put up a fight at Voronezh—which Timoshenko, recalling the plans taken from Major Reichel's grounded plane in June, knew to be Operation *Blau's* initial objective. So the bulk of the Fortieth Army was rounded up and headed east toward Voronezh with all possible speed.

Timoshenko's precipitous retreat jeopardized the whole first phase of Operation *Blau,* and one German general was quick to recognize that fact. He was Lieut. General Leo Geyr von Schweppenburg, who had replaced Stumme in command of the 40th Panzer Corps. What is more, General Geyr, as he was commonly called, conceived of a countermove. He immediately sought permission to turn the 40th Panzer Corps directly east toward the Don, where he might still cut off the fleeing Soviets. But General Paulus disliked field improvisations and denied the request. The answer Geyr got from Sixth Army headquarters merely repeated his original assignment: "40th Panzer Corps will turn northward in order to link up with Fourth Panzer Army."

By July 3, even Hitler had realized that Paulus was prob-

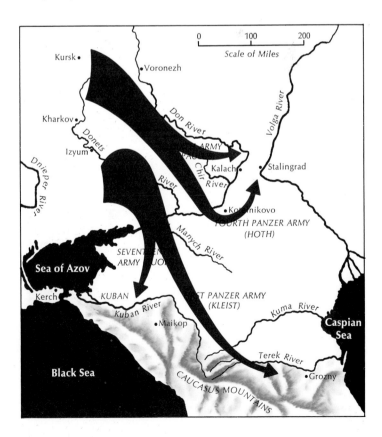

Operation Blau—Hitler's grandiose military scheme for the summer of 1942—envisoned an offensive on two major fronts. In the north, Army Group B—comprising General Paulus' Sixth Army and General Hoth's Fourth Panzer Army—was to clamp an iron vice on the city of Stalingrad from the north and south by advancing across the Don River and by curling up from the Kotelnikovo area. While the northern flank was being thus secured, Army Group A—General von Kleist's First Panzer Army and General Richard Ruoff's Seventeenth Army—was to sweep southward and capture the critical Caucasus oil fields at Grozny and Maikop.

A YOUTHFUL CITY ON THE EVE OF BATTLE

A handsome park graces a Stalingrad neighborhood; gardens were often shaped like the Red Star.

Heavy farm tractors roll from a giant assembly plant

"Stalingrad, city of our youth! Amidst the flowering of its hopes our youth has built and beautified this city. Here on the bank of the Volga they dreamed, hoped, loved. All they hold dear and beautiful is associated with this sun-flooded city."

These passionate lines, written in 1942 by two provincial officials, expressed far more than purely local pride. To Russians everywhere, Stalingrad was a special city—linked to youth in many ways.

It was as young as the Soviet epoch, having been rebuilt almost entirely after the civil war on the site of a 17th Century fortress named Tsaritsyn. The young had actually helped to build Comrade Stalin's namesake city; 7,000 Komsomols—members of the Communist Union of Youth—did much of the physical labor that raised the enormous tractor factory, one of the largest tractor plants west of the Urals. Other newly built factories in Stalingrad and several new trade schools—attracted young people from all over the U.S.S.R.

The 500,000 citizens of Stalingrad were young in their ideas as well as their Communist ideals. Scores of American engineers and architects were brought in to advise in the construction of the industrial

before its wartime conversion to tank production.

A Stalingrad bus, part of a metro system that included several tram lines, rolls past workers' apartments.

complexes. Young women, who dressed and labored like men within the factories, made regular visits to beauty parlors for manicures and permanents. Trucks fitted out as mobile soda fountains toured the city, and at dances Russian couples performed a step known as the Boston.

Everything in Stalingrad worked astonishingly well, even the various Five-Year Plans. Workers' apartments were erected on schedule. Machine shops, steel plants, textile mills, shipyards on the Volga and great collective farms in the surrounding countryside poured high-quality products into the Soviet economy. Yet the Stalingraders made time for musical and theatrical events at a giant opera house, and for civic-minded volunteer work.

In August of 1942, the people of Stalingrad knew that German armies were closing in on their city. But they went on with their work in their normal, bustling way. One woman, pausing to converse with an American journalist, prophesied the best and worst. "We cannot be conquered," she said. "The fathers of our children may die. Most of us may die. But we shall teach the German cannibals a lesson they won't forget—a lesson in steel and blood."

Cranes load barges on the Volga. Riverboats like the one at right carried a steady stream of visitors.

ably wasting time and fuel in his attempt to trap the Soviet armies near Voronezh. On that day, the Führer flew into Field Marshal von Bock's field headquarters and grandly informed him of a brand new plan for Voronezh: "I no longer insist on the capture of the town, Bock. Nor, indeed, do I consider it necessary. You are free, if you wish, to drive southward at once."

That change of mind set off a bewildering succession of orders, which, by the time it was over, would throw Operation *Blau* into complete disarray.

First, late on July 3, the 40th Panzer Corps's Geyr received a Sixth Army order reversing the earlier instructions and ordering him to head for the Don—just as he had previously requested in vain. No sooner had he started than, at noon the next day, the order was countermanded and he was again told to move toward Voronezh to cover the flank of the Fourth Panzer Army during its attack on the town. What had happened was that Bock, at last given the discretion so long denied by Hitler, had at first decided to bypass Voronezh; then, on learning that elements of his northern force were within two miles of the city, he had shifted gears in an effort to take Voronezh on the run.

It did not work out nearly like that. Instead, to his considerable confusion, Bock found Voronezh filled with Soviet troops, who had just arrived and were in troublesome humor. Those forces—the better part of nine rifle divisions, four rifle brigades, seven armored brigades and two antitank brigades—fought well enough to win the time necessary for the eventual salvation of Stalingrad. Not until July 13 did Bock manage to clear the place. Even then, he took precious few prisoners, and the Russians still clung to the vital supply road and railway on the east side of the Don.

On that same day, July 13, Hitler made perhaps the most disastrous decision in a career liberally sprinkled with disastrous decisions. Although his armies had met staunch opposition only at Voronezh, the timetable for *Blau* had been thrown utterly out of synchronization. To make up for lost time, he abandoned his carefully worked-out plan to settle matters in the north before opening the campaign in the south. Instead, he now resolved to seal off Stalingrad with one arm and, simultaneously, with the other arm, to unlock the gateway to the Caucasus by capturing Rostov.

Toward that end, General Ewald von Kleist's First Panzer Army, which according to the original plan had been expected to form the southern prong of the pincers against the Stalingrad area, was ordered to avoid Stalingrad and move immediately south toward Rostov. Even more significantly, General Hermann Hoth's Fourth Panzer Army, scheduled to stiffen the Sixth Army in its march on Stalingrad, was now diverted southward to assist Kleist.

Before that ill-starred day was gone, Bock had protested the division of his forces—and had been sacked. He was replaced by General Maximilian von Weichs. Yet the perils of the division were predictable to almost everyone but Hitler. The splitting of forces required a splitting of supplies, and since the armies attacking Rostov on the way into the Caucasus had the greater distance to travel, they received the larger share of ammunition and fuel. Stalingrad, Kleist wrote later, could have been taken "without a fight at the end of July." But Paulus, deprived of fuel by Hitler's decision, failed to meet that deadline—and in each day of delay, the Soviet defenses of Stalingrad improved.

Similarly, the Soviet defenses deep in the Caucasus were being improved while the Red Army defenders fought a delaying action at Rostov. The battle for that city began on July 22, and it was a vicious one.

The Germans at Rostov fared well at first. But after bursting through the city's recently constructed outer defenses with surprising ease, they found themselves plagued by NKVD troops and engineers, many of them veterans of insurrectionary street fighting. The Soviets sniped and hurled Molotov cocktails from balconies and rooftops; the streets were barricaded with paving stones and studded with steel girders planted on end as antitank obstacles; doorways were booby-trapped and every alley, it seemed, was planted with deadly mines.

"The fighting for the city center of Rostov was a merciless struggle," recalled German Colonel Alfred Reinhardt. "The defenders would not allow themselves to be taken alive: They fought to their last breath; and when they had been bypassed unnoticed, or wounded, they would still fire from behind cover until they were themselves killed. Our own wounded had to be placed in armored troop carriers and guarded—otherwise we would find them beaten or stabbed to death."

Reinhardt's regiment of the 125th Infantry Division handled the enemy coolly and methodically. After Rostov had been thoroughly torn up by a heavy artillery bombardment, the inner city was divided into four east-west sectors, designated A, B, C and D. Six assault companies, each with one heavy machine gun, one antitank gun, one infantry gun and one light field howitzer, attacked from north to south in line abreast, stopping at each of the sector boundaries to close and dress their ranks. Behind them came six cleanup companies, searching every building and routing out the soldiers and civilians, including women and children, whom the assault units had missed. One after another, zones A, B, C and D were cleared of defenders.

By July 24, the job was done. On that day the first German units crossed the Don at Rostov. Ahead of them lay 300 miles of open steppe—and the Caucasus.

Meanwhile, Paulus and his Sixth Army kept on advancing—and finding virtually no one to fight. Back at Wehrmacht headquarters, Chief of the General Staff Halder worriedly followed the Sixth Army's unopposed progress down the Don toward Kalach, where a key bridge offered the best opportunity for a river crossing on the way to Stalingrad. "The Russians are systematically avoiding contact, my Führer," he told Hitler. "Nonsense," scoffed Hitler. "The Russians are in full flight. They are reeling from the blows we have dealt them during the past few months." But Halder remained gravely concerned, confiding to his diary that Hitler's "persistent underestimation of the enemy's potential is gradually taking on grotesque forms."

Up to a point, Hitler was right about the Soviet condition. A controlled retreat was perhaps the most difficult of all military maneuvers for even the best-trained troops—and the Russians were much less than that. Timoshenko's withdrawal order had been badly drafted and was taken by tens of thousands of Red Army soldiers as a signal to run for their lives. Thus, while some divisions marched steadily toward Stalingrad, others fled in wild disorder. To stem the tide of panicked troops, Major General V. Ya. Kolpakchy, the commander of the Sixty-second Army, stationed his staff officers—armed with submachine guns—near the Kalach bridge. Besides stopping Russian runaways, they anxiously scanned the horizon expecting Paulus to appear at any moment with the Sixth Army.

But the Sixth Army failed to arrive, and Kolpakchy soon signaled Timoshenko, "The Germans are not following up."

"What does it mean?" Timoshenko asked his chief of staff. "Have the Germans changed their plans?"

Not this time. In fact, the fuel tanks of Paulus' panzers had finally run dry. The Sixth Army had come to a dead stop approximately 150 miles short of Kalach, and there it remained for 18 days.

Timoshenko was quick to grasp at what he supposed was a rare opportunity. "If the Germans are not following up," he told staff officers, "there is time to organize the defense on the western bank of the Don." Without further ado, he poured into the great bend of the Don around Kalach all the elements he could round up of four armies, along with two tank armies still in the process of formation.

By thus cramming his masses into a narrow front, without room to maneuver, Timoshenko committed his worst and certainly his last blunder in a major combat command. When the Sixth Army's fuel was finally replenished, Paulus came with a rush in a classic double envelopment. His 14th Panzer Corps swung out from his left and the 24th Panzer Corps, on loan from Hoth's Fourth Panzer Army, wheeled around from his right. On August 8, when the pincers closed, more than 70,000 Soviet troops, about 1,000 tanks and armored vehicles, and 750 guns were trapped within the Kalach pocket.

For all practical purposes, the way had been cleared to Stalingrad. Yet after that furious burst of energy, Paulus spent nearly two weeks tidying up around Kalach and waiting for Hoth, who had finally been recalled by Hitler, to work his way back up from the south. Only on August 21 did Sixth Army units at last cross the Don and gather for the lunge toward the Volga.

The Red Army had been granted barely enough time to regroup yet again and to gird for its fight for survival at Stalingrad.

ON THE ROAD TO STALINGRAD

German motorcyclists reconnoiter the burning steppe en route to Stalingrad in 1942. Luftwaffe incendiary bombs had ignited the grass to flush out Soviet troops.

THE SIXTH ARMY'S LAGGARDLY ADVANCE

Never had a German army in enemy territory put on a spectacle quite like the march that took the Sixth Army the last 40 miles from the Don River to Stalingrad in the final week of August 1942. It was not so much a military operation as a rambling, light-hearted, almost casual stroll across the Russian steppe.

As they broke bivouac for the journey, the 250,000 soldiers were supremely confident of victory. Indeed, this army had experienced nothing else. Known as the Tenth Army in 1939, it had slashed through Poland, giving the world a first terrifying glimpse of blitzkrieg. Then, as the Sixth Army, it had campaigned gloriously through the Netherlands, Belgium and France. Most recently, it had easily smashed Soviet forces west of the Don, taking 57,000 prisoners and putting the remnants of two armies to flight. The troops had no reason to think that Stalingrad would be any different; that city was—as one of their generals later said—"no more than a name on the map to us."

The mighty army—20 divisions with 500 tanks, 7,000 guns and mortars, and 25,000 horses—advanced across the hot, dusty land on a broad front. The far-flung columns traveled in fits and starts. They paused from time to time to accept the surrender of Red Army stragglers, some of whom came in driving their tanks. The fine dust caused delays—fouling motors and forcing German vehicles to pull over for repairs. There were also waits for gasoline, which had to be brought up on a supply line stretching more than 300 miles to the nearest depots in the Stalino area. It was just as well that the Sixth Army's commander, Lieut. General Friedrich Paulus, was in no hurry. He thought Stalingrad would fall in a day.

In overnight camps, the soldiers kept telling one another that "*Russland ist kaputt,*" and talking about the jobs they would get as soon as the War ended. The Wehrmacht's highly vaunted discipline was so relaxed that upon reaching the Volga River north of Stalingrad, panzer troops stripped off their grimy clothes and dived into the cold water. But then the brief vacation from battle ended with the rumble of gunfire from Stalingrad.

General Friedrich Paulus, wearing gloves and dust goggles, indicates a line of advance from a forward position as his Sixth Army nears Stalingrad.

Symbol of the Soviet retreat from the Don to the Volga, a tank lies crippled and abandoned in a field of sunflowers, raised for fodder in the Stalingrad area.

Caked with dust, a German motorcyclist peers ahead through heavy goggles. The clouds of dust raised by advancing German units darkened the skies for miles around.

From his position on a cliff high above the Don River, a German machine gunner guards against any attack by enemy rear-guard units on the Wehrmacht crossing points.

Crowding the river's edge, a German unit gets ready to paddle across the Don in rubber dinghies. But the bulk of the Sixth Army used pontoon bridges to make the crossing.

German troops rush to cut the Tula railway, Stalingrad's last link to Moscow. Luftwaffe bombs had silenced nearby Soviet opposition.

Moving up supplies, a group of horsemen from a German division overtakes a truck convoy stalled for lack of fuel in a village on the steppe.

Hitching a ride on top of an assault gun, panzer grenadiers wear ponchos against one of the infrequent rain showers rolling across the steppe during the dry summer months.

A tank crewman carries two cans of scarce gas from a supply truck to his panzer, and in the process fuels himself with a chunk of bread.

Accompanied by their horse-drawn supply carts, German troops travel a dirt road scored by the treads of their armored vanguard.

In search of the elusive enemy, two infantrymen share a cigarette in a deep ravine typical of the gorges that crisscrossed the steppe.

Fleeing the Germans, women and children in the Stalingrad area pull carts laden with possessions to ferries that will take them to safety across the Volga. Peasants from nearby farms took their livestock with them.

Crouched in a shell hole on the outskirts of Stalingrad, a German noncom urges his troops forward. The bolt on his submachine gun is open, indicating that he has encountered resistance and has fired a clip.

4

Lieut. General Friedrich Paulus, destined to lead more than 200,000 Germans to death or captivity, was a handsome man with fastidious ways. He habitually wore gloves—not just because of his taste for military swank but because he detested dirt. Throughout his long career as a staff officer, Paulus took pains to bathe and change his uniform twice a day. Because of his cleanly splendor, certain officers sarcastically dubbed him "The Noble Lord" or "Our Most Elegant Gentleman."

Yet despite a certain appearance of aristocratic dash, Paulus came from a thoroughly bourgeois family and apparently was happiest with staff work. The son of a Hessian bookkeeper, he entered the Army in 1910 as a 19-year-old cadet officer, did staff work throughout World War I and, although attrition created numerous opportunities for advancement, he emerged as a mere captain. After the War, when the Army was small and promotions few and far between, a superior officer took Paulus' measure: "He is slow, but very methodical in his office work and is passionately interested in war games, both on the map and the sand model." But action in the field was something else. During maneuvers in the mid-1920s, when Paulus was unexpectedly required to command an infantry regiment in an exercise, his performance was found wanting. "This officer," wrote the director of the war games, "lacks decisiveness."

As of January 30, 1933, when Adolf Hitler took power as Chancellor of Germany, Paulus was a major in his 23rd year behind Wehrmacht desks. Although he was indifferent to politics, Paulus quickly convinced himself that Hitler was invincible as a military leader. His faith in Hitler was blind—and a certain recommendation for rapid advancement in Nazi Germany.

And so, during the course of the next few years, Paulus was repeatedly promoted for his solid if unexceptional staff work. By September of 1939, he was a major general and the chief of staff of the German Tenth Army (later reorganized as the Sixth Army) under General Walther von Reichenau during the invasion of Poland. The two of them worked well together, perhaps because Reichenau was everything that Paulus was not. Reichenau was a boisterous bear of a man whose disdain for desk work was matched only by his superb abilities as a fighting commander. Although their close professional relationship lasted for only a few months,

THE WAR OF THE RATS

Reichenau was soon to play a pivotal part in Paulus' life.

In September of 1940, Paulus, by now deputy chief of the German General Staff, was hard at work planning Operation *Barbarossa*, the invasion of Russia. Elated by the offensive he worked out on his maps and sand models, he predicted, "It is possible even that the campaign will be all over in from four to six weeks."

Not quite. But as it turned out, Paulus benefited from the Wehrmacht's failure to win a quick victory. On the 30th of November, 1941, Field Marshal Gerd von Rundstedt had been sacked for his protests against orders requiring him to hold out against Russian forces that threatened to encircle elements of his Army Group South. On December 3, over a vegetarian dinner of potato puffs, millet and pumpkin at Poltava, the new commander of Army Group South—Reichenau himself—suggested to Hitler that his quiet, plodding former chief of staff succeed him as commander of the Sixth Army. Paulus, having long aspired to a field command, was delighted to learn of his new appointment.

Undoubtedly Reichenau meant to help Paulus until he was comfortable in his new post. But on January 12, even as Paulus assumed command, Reichenau suffered a heart attack and died five days later in a plane crash while he was being flown to Leipzig for treatment. Paulus, who had never led a single soldier into battle, found himself alone at the head of an army.

At this critical moment for the Sixth Army, the officer who had become Paulus' first chief of staff, Colonel Ferdinand Heim, drew a penetrating word picture of the new commander: "a slender, rather over-tall figure, whose slight stoop seemed somehow to be a gesture of good will toward those of smaller stature. Was it the face of an ascetic? For that it was hardly severe enough. Rather, I would say, it was the face of a martyr."

This, then, was the man who on August 22, 1942, sent a Sixth Army tank column stabbing from the banks of the Don toward the crucible at Stalingrad *(map, page 139)*.

Stalingrad, a provincial center of 500,000 inhabitants, was the Soviet Union's third largest industrial city, producing more than a quarter of the Red Army's tanks and other mechanized vehicles. To the Germans, it was a most inviting target. A narrow ribbon of a city, stretching more than 30 miles along the precipitous west bank of the mile-wide Volga River, it could be snipped with ease at almost any point—or so the attackers believed.

To the north, the city was built around four tremendous industrial complexes. Northernmost was the old Stalingrad tractor factory, which before the War had made 10,000 farm tractors a year; now it was cranking out tanks. The plant sprawled for a mile along the main north-south road into Stalingrad and was fronted to the west by a workers' paradise—more than 300 rent-free apartment buildings, some of them six stories high. They were part of a self-contained community with its own stores, schools, movie theater, circus and soccer fields.

To the south lay two complexes named in honor of the Revolution: the Barricades plant, which produced arms and ammunition, and below it the Red October steelworks, block upon block of foundries and assembly plants that manufactured small arms. The southernmost factory was the Lazur chemical plant, around whose yellow brick buildings looped a railroad track; the enclosed area was to become known for its shape as the "tennis racket." Each one of these factory areas would soon become a scene of enormous carnage and ruin.

Another battlefield, lying just south and west of the factory district, loomed 330 feet above the plateau on which Stalingrad stood. This was Mamayev Hill, an ancient Tartar burial mound now used for picnics. It was designated on military maps as Hill 102, but it would be known and feared as the "Iron Heights" by the men of both armies who scratched and clawed for its summit.

The heart of Stalingrad, Red Square, featured a fountain with a curious statuary display of children dancing around a crocodile. Around the square were government buildings, *Pravda's* offices, the Gorky Theater and the Univermag Department Store. All were squat. All were ugly. All would be smashed by German bombs during the first 48 hours of the battle for Stalingrad. The entire central district was cut by a series of deep ravines—carved out of the red earth by small east-west Volga tributaries—which served as barriers to north-south military movement. One of these, the 200-foot-deep Tsaritsa Gorge, wound its way past what would later become two key German objectives: Railroad Station No. 1 and the main ferry landing for traffic across the Volga.

The southern section of Stalingrad was the avenue by which Paulus would seek to seize the city. It was a beehive of workers' homes, most of them little wooden cottages; here and there rose the bulbous onion-shaped spires of the Russian Orthodox churches. The district seemed to present no serious challenge. The German planners took little account of a towering concrete grain elevator that stood near the dividing line between the southern and central sectors of Stalingrad.

According to the plans worked out with Army Group B for the Stalingrad campaign, Paulus would send the Sixth Army's 14th Panzer Corps—three divisions under General Gustav von Wietersheim—lancing across the flat, 40-mile corridor between the Don and the Volga. It would thrust through Stalingrad's northern suburbs and penetrate to the Volga itself; there the corps would face south, using the river to anchor its left flank, and set up an unbreakable blocking position. Next, the 10 divisions of General Hermann Hoth's elite Fourth Panzer Army would strike the southern district and drive north along the Volga, rolling over the Russians in Stalingrad. Finally, the Sixth Army's six infantry divisions would attack from the west, driving into the city on a broad front, shoving any remaining Russians into the Volga.

The plan looked perfect on paper, and Paulus was excited by the prospects. "The great thing now," he wrote, "is to hit the Russian so hard a crack that he won't recover for a very long time." All in all, he reckoned, this might be accomplished within a week.

Instead, the struggle for Stalingrad lasted more than five months, turning into a titanic test of wills between Hitler and Stalin. At first, Hitler had viewed Stalingrad as secondary to his thrust into the Caucasus, while Stalin had been so certain the enemy would strike elsewhere that he had held his reserves far to the north. But for several reasons, both dictators changed their minds.

Stalingrad had held a special attraction for Stalin ever since the Russian civil war, when it was known as Tsaritsyn.

In June of 1918, People's Commissar Stalin had meddled in the defense of the city while on an assignment in the south to expedite grain shipments to a starving Moscow. Finding Tsaritsyn in turmoil because of attacks by White Army Cossacks, Stalin had instituted Draconian measures.

Before long, the corpses of citizens whom he had condemned as political subversives were being dumped nightly from a barge moored in the great river. Tsaritsyn remained Red throughout the four months Stalin spent there, and even though it fell to White Army forces a year later, Stalin thenceforth insisted that his defense of the city had been the turning point of the Bolshevik Revolution. By 1925, he was powerful enough to honor the city by naming it after himself. And in 1942, he had no intention of dishonoring his namesake by letting it fall into German hands.

More important, Stalin felt that the loss of Stalingrad would give the German attackers the option of wheeling north toward Moscow or south toward the Caucasus, and that it would convince the Western Allies that the Soviet Union was lost. So the Soviet dictator soon issued the grim directive: "Not one step backward. The Volga has now only one bank."

Hitler, on the other hand, would refuse to admit that his attack on Stalingrad was a mistake. As soon as his armies ran into trouble in the city, he would make it impossible to back off later by boasting to the German people, "You may rest assured that nobody will ever drive us out of Stalingrad." The city would become an obsession to him, and when Russian power threatened to recapture it, the Führer would cry, "I am not leaving the Volga!"

Thus Stalingrad attained a symbolic importance far in excess of its considerable strategic value as a site commanding the whole immense Volga basin between Moscow and Baku on the Caspian Sea. The clash for the city would exact a colossal toll. More than one million soldiers and civilians—men, women and children, Germans, Russians, Italians, Hungarians and Rumanians—would die at the lowest and cruelest level of the human condition. The Germans had a word for it: *Rattenkrieg* (War of the Rats).

On the parched afternoon of August 22, 1942, pleasant thoughts of an easy victory at Stalingrad ran through the mind of Lieut. General Hans Hube, an old infantry soldier who had lost his left arm in World War I. General Hube was a hard fighter, and his troops paid him the considerable compliment of calling him, simply, *der Mensch* (the Man). Now, as commander of the 16th Panzer Division, the striking tip of General von Wietersheim's 14th Panzer

Corps, Hube was preparing to lead the Sixth Army's rush from the Don to the Volga.

German infantry units had just crossed the Don and established bridgeheads in the neighboring villages at Vertyachy and Luchinskoi. Near the pontoon bridge at Vertyachý, Hube knelt in a peasant's garden, a battle map spread on the ground before him. He liked what he saw. "There are no streams or ravines crossing our line of advance," he said to one of his unit commanders. "Here's our opportunity to drive a corridor right through the enemy to the Volga in one fell swoop." A few moments later a motorcycle dispatch-rider pulled up bearing the attack orders. Hube quickly glanced at the paper and said, "The balloon goes up at 0430 hours tomorrow." To one of his departing commanders, the general gave a stirring send-off: "Tomorrow night in Stalingrad!"

That night Hube's tanks began clanking across the Don and into the Luchinskoi bridgehead, an area about three miles wide and one and a half miles deep. By midnight many were in place, ready to start their plunge toward Stalingrad. Under a thunderous bombardment from Russian planes and artillery, the panzer grenadiers—heavily armed infantrymen who accompanied the tanks—dug their foxholes and went to sleep.

The 16th Panzer Division rolled forward at first light on August 23. Survivors of the outfit would long remember the wild beauty of that morning—the predawn gray pierced first by bolts of orange, violet and red light and then suffused with the unbroken ruddy brilliance of the sun. Behind Hube's outfit, the main body of Paulus' Sixth Army lurched forward. But it soon lagged far behind, slowed down by fuel shortages and its own dawdling in the expectation of an easy victory.

Hube rode in the command vehicle of the signal corps company, crackling out orders; his signalmen handled more than 450 messages that day. Ahead, he had judged, lay ideal tank country, flat and barren of impeding woodlands. The steppe, rainless for two months, was soon baking in temperatures above 100° F., and the tankers gazed longingly at the watermelon patches outside villages along the way. The tanks raised great plumes of dust that were wafted toward Stalingrad by the arid westerly wind. Stuka dive bombers returning from the city—the Luftwaffe flew some 2,000

sorties that day—dipped low over the tank columns, their sirens screaming in triumph.

The steppe bristled with Soviet opposition—but only on maps. In fact, the Russian Sixty-second Army had been severely mauled in the fighting west of the Don. Now, in confusion, most of its shattered units were fleeing toward what they supposed was safety in Stalingrad. The Russians made one attempt to stop the Germans at the Tartar Ditch, an ancient defensive rampart between the Don and the Volga, but Hube's tanks burst through the earthen walls as if they were made of papier-mâché. Scattered pockets of resistance were spotted by German reconnaissance planes, marked by smoke bombs and quickly exterminated by combat teams that peeled off from the main tank columns. In the early afternoon, the commander of Hube's leading tank announced, much in the manner of a tour guide, over

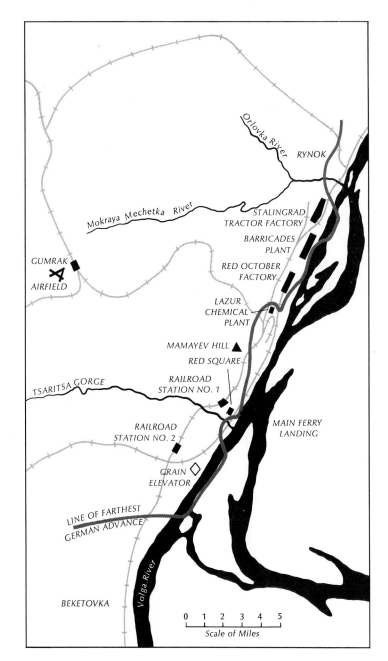

Though every building, every barricaded street corner and square, every hill and ravine in Stalingrad became a fortress, the main defenses were concentrated on Mamayev Hill in the center of the city and on the line of industrial plants and railroad stations running north and south of the hill. At the climax of the German advance, the Russians were driven from virtually all their strong points, and they clung precariously to only a few footholds on the banks of the Volga. The most critical of these was the main ferry landing, where supplies and reinforcements came from across the river; without this the defenders would have been doomed.

his throat microphone: "Over on the right, the skyline of Stalingrad."

As Hube's tanks neared Rynok, Stalingrad's northernmost suburb beyond the factory district, they came under massed artillery fire from their right. The shelling was remarkably inaccurate, and the tanks briskly turned to deal with the nuisance. One by one they knocked out the emplacements —37 in all—and then stopped to inspect the damage they had inflicted. Strewn about the batteries were the twisted corpses of the gunners. They were workers from the Barricades factory—and they were women.

As evening fell, Hube's lead elements rumbled through the streets of Rynok and arrived at the cliff-sided west bank of the Volga. Gazing out at the river, the German invaders saw scores of boats scurrying below, cutting white wakes through the darkening yellow water. The Stukas, for all their siren-screams of triumph, had notably failed to halt traffic on the river, Stalingrad's lifeline for supplies and reinforcements from the east bank. Until the Germans could cut off this traffic, Stalingrad would remain alive.

Yet at this moment, it hardly seemed to matter. In the gathering darkness, Hube swung his tanks into a circular hedgehog defense perimeter and awaited the next day in full confidence that he could then fight his way at least as far south as the tractor factory, thereby widening his corridor and consolidating his blocking position.

That night, from their camp amid the vineyards and chestnut trees on the Volga's west bank, Hube's men witnessed a spectacular display of fireworks. In the heaviest Luftwaffe raid in more than a year, General Wolfram von Richthofen (cousin of the World War I ace) threw against Stalingrad every available plane of his 8th Air Corps, including even bomb-carrying Ju-52 transport squadrons. Six hundred planes in all flew at least one sortie. The terror raid—more than half the bombs were incendiaries—threw up walls of flame by whose light a newspaper could be read halfway back to the Don. The raid killed tens of thousands of civilians. When the bombing ended, Richthofen contentedly wrote in his diary: "We simply paralyzed the Russians."

Next morning Hube launched his 16th Panzer Division toward the tractor factory. He pushed to within a half-mile of his goal. But then he was stopped cold by a storm of Soviet metal from a nearby hill. Overnight, the Russians had

managed to establish a defense line of militiamen, women and units of the Sixty-second Army. Brand new T-34 tanks, their hulls still unpainted, rolled straight into the battle from the assembly lines of the tractor factory, with many of them driven by the very workers who had made them.

On August 25, Hube renewed his attack but made no progress. Worse, Soviet forces were closing in behind him, cutting his supply line. Suddenly, Hube's position was becoming perilous. During his initial rush across the steppe, he had outdistanced the rest of the Sixth Army. He was already in need of supplies and reinforcements, and any relief column would have to fight its way through the barrier of Soviet forces, which were steadily being strengthened.

Hube fought for four days, suffering heavy losses. By August 29, his troops had been driven back and penned up along a three-mile stretch of the Volga. The division still had received no supplies, no reinforcements.

Hube looked for a way out. "Our only chance," he said, "is to break through to the west"—away from the Volga and Stalingrad. But Hitler's orders were inflexible. "The 16th Panzer," he had signaled, "will hold its positions in all circumstances." Thus, Hube had to cling to the ground he held and wait for the rest of his corps to break through the Soviet line between them.

Meanwhile, the southern attack by General Hoth's Fourth Panzer Army had gotten off to a slow start. This in itself was ominous, for Hermann Hoth was the sort of general who could be counted on to get the job done. Like Hube, he was a tough former infantryman who ranked with the best of the tank experts. Like Hube, he had had a nickname bestowed upon him by his admiring troops. Although his appearance was forbidding—his eyes cold, his nose accipitrine, his mouth hard—the men called him "Papa." And like Hube, Hoth in those days of August was a thoroughly frustrated German general.

The trouble was that the High Command could not make up its mind what to do with the Fourth Panzer Army. First, in July 1942, Hoth had been sent off by Hitler on a superfluous mission to help General von Kleist's First Panzer Army cross the lower Don on the way to the Caucasus. There he had met with a cool reception. "I did not need its aid," Kleist later said of Hoth's army, "and it simply congested the roads." Hoth then was recalled for the attack on Stalingrad, but was required to leave behind one of his two panzer corps for the Caucasus campaign. Thus, on August 20, he found himself understrength, still 20 miles short of the target city and confronted by some of the worst tank terrain he had ever seen: deep ravines guarding the approaches to a line of hills that commanded the bend of the Volga south of Stalingrad.

Hoth drove head-on at the hills, only to discover that the area was occupied in force by several tank-supported divisions of the Soviet Sixty-fourth Army, a seasoned formation under the command of Major General M. S. Shumilov. Hoth was thrown back.

Hoth tried again, and again, and still again. He lost the commander of the 24th Panzer Regiment. He lost the commander of the 21st Panzer Grenadier Regiment. He lost thousands of men of lesser rank. He lost more tanks than he cared to count. Finally, a few days later with the hills still a good distance away, Hoth took cover in one of the ravines and conferred with his chief of staff. "We've got to tackle this thing differently," he said. "We are merely bleeding ourselves white in front of these damned hills; that's no ground for armor. We must regroup and mount our attack somewhere else, somewhere a long way from here."

Hoth did precisely that, and with consummate skill, during the next two nights. Masking his intentions by shifting infantry units to the front, he pulled his tanks out of the line and swung them 30 miles to the south and west, taking up a position from which he could outflank and bypass those "damned hills." On August 29, the same day Hube spoke anxiously of breaking away from the Volga, Hoth struck northward with devastating effect. On August 30, his advance units ripped through Stalingrad's inner ring of fortifications at Gavrilovka. On August 31, Hoth's tanks and troops slashed 20 miles to the Stalingrad-Karpovak railroad line and threatened to drive a wedge into the Soviet Sixty-second and Sixty-fourth Armies. Now, if only Paulus would move swiftly, swinging the remainder of the Sixth Army south to join with Hoth, huge Soviet concentrations might be cut off.

At Army Group B headquarters, General von Weichs recognized the possibilities and signaled to Paulus: "Everything now depends on Sixth Army launching an attack in a general southerly direction in order to destroy the enemy forces west of Stalingrad in cooperation with the Fourth Panzer Army. This decision requires the ruthless denuding of secondary fronts."

It was a glorious opportunity—but Paulus was not the man to seize it. Mulling over his maps, fretting over his shaky northern flank, he hesitated for three days before making his move to join up with Hoth. By then, the Russians had retreated into Stalingrad. The Soviet commander there had been given priceless time for rigging his defenses.

That commander was Lieut. General Andrei Ivanovich Yeremenko, a thickset man with shoulders like slabs of beef. Yeremenko had won his commission in the Revolution, and before the war with Germany he had commanded the crack

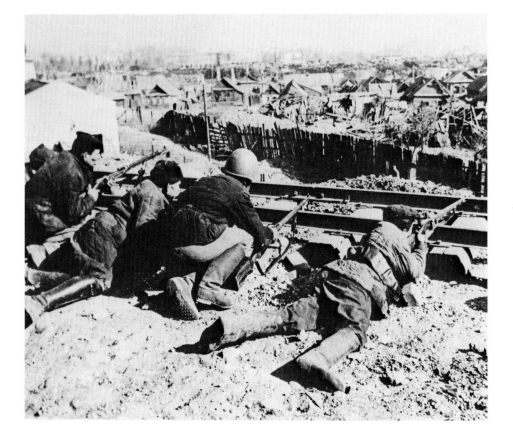

Steadying their rifles on a railroad track, factory workers in Stalingrad prepare to defend their homes at the edge of the industrial district. By early September, 1942, two weeks after the German onslaught began, 7,000 factory hands had been drafted into fighting squads.

Special Red Banner Far Eastern Army, charged with guarding the border against attack by the Japanese in Manchuria. He had suffered a leg wound in the fighting on the central front and was still recovering on August 2 when Stalin had summoned him without explanation to his private quarters in the Kremlin. Yeremenko had been appropriately wary when he arrived, and he was vastly relieved to find the dictator in a genial mood.

"Do you consider yourself recovered?" Stalin had asked. "Yes," said Yeremenko. But another general in attendance had noticed that Yeremenko was still limping somewhat and said, "It looks like his wound is still bothering him." Stalin replied coldly, "We shall consider that Comrade Yeremenko has fully recovered." And that settled that. "Due to the circumstances around Stalingrad," Stalin continued, "prompt action must be taken to fortify this most important sector of the front."

Hurrying to Stalingrad, Yeremenko found himself teamed with Nikita Khrushchev, who was known as one of the ablest of the political commissars. At the moment, however, Khrushchev's reputation was tarnished and he was in disgrace: He had been involved in the Russian disaster at Kharkov and was fortunate to escape Stalin's usual penalty for failure—arrest or worse. Now, desperately eager to redeem himself, he threw all his abundant energies into working with Yeremenko to save Stalingrad.

On August 4, the two took up headquarters in a bunker that had been dug into the wall of the Tsaritsa Gorge. The bunker was of somewhat mysterious prewar origin; no one seemed to know how it got there, or why. Khrushchev, for one, was convinced that Stalin had ordered it built for his own future use. The refuge, Khrushchev wrote years later, "was decorated very much according to Stalin's taste. The walls had oak plywood trimming, just like all of Stalin's *dachas*. The place was very well equipped. It was even fitted out with a toilet."

Despite Khrushchev's help, Yeremenko could scarcely begin to cope with the problems he faced. Stalin, suspecting that the Germans would attack farther north, had sent capable leaders to Stalingrad but too few followers. Though new units were beginning to arrive, Yeremenko was short of troops, short of ordnance, short of supplies.

But Yeremenko did what he could. He set Stalingrad's civilian population to constructing a makeshift defense perimeter. Much more important, he reckoned that the most dangerous enemy thrust would come from his left, so he shifted Sixty-fourth Army units and all the artillery he could muster to the line of hills south of Stalingrad. It was a brilliant move, for there they successfully blunted the initial drive of Hoth's Fourth Panzer Army.

Hoth's attack from the south was a serious threat, and it spread confusion through the Soviet ranks. When the Germans struck on the morning of August 23, frantic telephone calls began coming into Yeremenko's bunker from Russian outposts along the 16th Panzer Division's line of assault. At one point, a major general called in to report the destruction of a small supply depot out on the steppe. Enraged by the man's excitement over a picayune matter, Yeremenko shouted, "Carry on with your job. Stop this panic."

Khrushchev soon arrived at the bunker from his downtown apartment and was quickly briefed by Yeremenko. "Very unpleasant facts," the commissar said coolly. "What can we do to keep them from Stalingrad?" While Yeremenko was explaining his efforts to reinforce the city's industrial district, the apparent German objective, two engineering officers entered the bunker. For days, they had been constructing a pontoon bridge across the mile-wide Volga, the only span that linked the east and west banks. Now the officers announced with pride that they had completed the job.

Yeremenko told them to go back and destroy the bridge. The officers stared at him as if he had taken leave of his senses. "Yes, yes," snapped Yeremenko, "I said to destroy it. And quickly." It was a difficult decision. But Yeremenko knew that his forces in the city would be greatly outnumbered by the Germans, that there was every chance of a breakthrough and that no bridge at all was better than one seized by the Germans.

Luftwaffe bombing raids that same day and night devastated Stalingrad. The municipal waterworks were smashed; henceforth firemen would be without water hookups in the midst of a city aflame. The *Pravda* building went down, then the telephone exchange, burying operators at their switchboards and knocking out regular telephone communications throughout the city. The commander of Stalingrad's

During a Luftwaffe bombing raid on Stalingrad, citizens and Red Army troops man an antiaircraft gun in the flaming central city. From late August of 1942 to February of 1943, the Luftwaffe flew more than 100,000 sorties over Stalingrad and dropped about 100,000 tons of bombs. This fierce bombardment, together with almost as many tons of artillery and mortar shells, left scarcely a building standing in the city.

military garrison deserted, throwing his men into confusion and leaving the city without effective crowd or traffic control. By dawn of August 24, the area around Red Square had been leveled and more than 100 blocks of downtown Stalingrad were burning. A bizarre note was added: A group of mental patients had walked out of their asylum during the bombing and wandered naked along the dry streambed at the bottom of a ravine.

Yeremenko used the day of the air raids to shore up his shaky defense line north of the tractor factory. One unit of 6,000 reinforcements was ferried across the Volga expecting to be employed in the southern sector; instead, as soon as the men set foot on dry ground, they were rushed north. Marines who had been called in from the Soviet Far East Fleet were packed into commandeered automobiles and, with their rifles bristling through the car windows, were driven full speed to join in the defense. When the 16th Panzer Division renewed its assault, Yeremenko's jerry-built northern line held—and continued to hold.

In that first week of fighting, not all of the Soviet units on the east bank of the Volga wanted to join the battle. At one point, stories of the horrors of the fighting in Stalingrad panicked the raw troops of the newly arrived 64th Infantry Division; they began deserting their assembly area by ones and by twos, then in dozens and in droves. To remedy the situation, the division commander called out his men and made a speech extolling the virtues of patriotism and denouncing the evils of cowardice. Then, to underscore his point, he began walking with pistol drawn down the front row of troops, counting as he went: "One, two, three, four. . . ." He shot the 10th man through the head and began again: "One, two, three, four. . . ." Six times he shot the 10th man through the head. After that, nobody had any complaints about the division's courage.

In the second week of September, the battle for Stalingrad took on a definitive shape. General Hoth's Fourth Panzer Army in the south, setting out on September 8 to make amends for Paulus' fatal hesitation, drove due east and reached the Volga below the grain elevator on September 10. The Soviet Sixty-second Army was now sealed in the city. But Hoth's drive stalled, and the battle line in the south—like the one above the tractor factory in the north—was more or less stabilized. Meanwhile, Paulus finally arrived and drew up the main body of his Sixth Army on a broad front along Stalingrad's western outskirts. From now on, Paulus' army would simply try to butt its way through the city—and through the Soviet Sixty-second Army.

As the opposing armies began grappling at close quarters,

Stalin nervously reshuffled his Stalingrad arrangements. On August 27, he had placed General Georgy Zhukov, the hero of Moscow, in charge of overall strategy for the Stalingrad area. Zhukov's great moments at Stalingrad would come later; for the time being he could do little but feed reinforcements into the battle or—even more important as the conflict developed—withhold his reserves for future use.

Meanwhile Yeremenko and Khrushchev found that they could not effectively control the entire front from their Tsaritsa bunker. Khrushchev therefore suggested during a phone conversation with Stalin that he and his military colleague move to the Volga's east bank. "No," replied Stalin, "that's impossible. If your troops find out that their commander has moved his headquarters out of Stalingrad, the city will fall." But Khrushchev finally prevailed with Stalin, and upon leaving took pleasure in tormenting one F. I. Golikov, a Stalin favorite who had been added to the Stalingrad team as Yeremenko's deputy commander.

According to Khrushchev's highly colored account, he informed Golikov that he was being left behind in Stalingrad. "A look of terror came over Golikov's face," Khrushchev later recalled with much relish, "but for the moment he contained himself. As soon as Yeremenko left the room, Golikov pleaded with me not to leave him alone in the city. I never saw anyone, soldier or civilian, in such a state during the whole war. He was white as a sheet and begged me not to abandon him. He kept saying over and over, 'Stalingrad is doomed! Don't leave me behind! Don't destroy me! Let me go with you!' A few days later we received a message from an officer in Stalingrad informing us that Golikov had gone completely off his head and was behaving like a madman. We relieved Golikov of his duties and had him recalled."

Poor Golikov was not the only ranking Soviet officer unmanned by the terrors of Stalingrad. Lieut. General Aleksandr I. Lopatin, commander of the Sixty-second Army, despaired of holding the city. When Lopatin announced his intention to abandon Stalingrad, Yeremenko immediately relieved him from command. In his place, with Stalin's permission, Yeremenko and Khrushchev on September 12 named the deputy commander of the Sixty-fourth Army, a previously obscure general named Vasily Ivanovich Chuikov—who, almost upon the instant of his accession, became the central figure of the battle of Stalingrad.

Chuikov was a peasant's son and looked it. He wore a uniform so rumpled that he was sometimes mistaken for an enlisted man. His unkept black hair kept falling over his forehead and his smile displayed rows of gold-capped teeth. In his boyhood he had been both a shop apprentice and a bellhop. But war was his natural element, and he had risen to regimental command in the fighting against the Whites. When the Germans launched *Barbarossa*, Chuikov was in Chungking, serving as a military adviser to Chiang Kai-shek as part of an old Sino-Russian agreement to oppose Japanese expansion. But nothing could keep him from the battle at home, or from making his presence felt. He was volatile, abrasive and ruthless, and it was much more than mere bombast when, on being offered the command of the Sixty-second Army on the 12th of September, he assured Yeremenko: "We shall hold the city or die there."

The latter alternative seemed far more likely. To hold a 20-mile line, Chuikov had an army of six divisions—approximately 55,000 troops, most of them still reeling from the retreat into Stalingrad. Gaping holes appeared in unit rosters. One regiment was down from 3,000 men to a forlorn 100. An infantry brigade, with a normal strength of 4,000 to 5,000, now counted exactly 666—of whom only 200 were qualified riflemen. A 10,000-man division now numbered 1,500. A tank brigade, normally 80 tanks strong, had been reduced to a lone tank. Against these ravaged forces, the Germans were tightening their grip on the city and preparing for a new offensive with some 100,000 men, 1,800 guns and 500 tanks, backed by more than 1,000 aircraft.

The very next morning after Chuikov took command, Paulus at last signaled the start of his belated offensive with a massive artillery bombardment. On September 13, under cover of his artillery, Paulus directed two sledgehammer blows at Stalingrad, with three infantry divisions from his main force attacking from the west and four of Hoth's divisions—two of them panzers—striking from the south. Paulus' primary objective was to take the central city, including Mamayev Hill and Railroad Station No. 1, then to break through to the Volga. All that day, the German forces ground forward against stiff resistance and edged into central Stalingrad. Before dawn on September 14, Chuikov, who had moved the Sixty-second Army headquarters from

Mamayev Hill to the Tsaritsa bunker, mounted a counterattack that made some headway. But, as he later wrote, "Once the sun had risen, German planes, in groups of 50 or 60, proceeded to bomb our counterattacking forces nonstop. Our counterattack failed."

The German forces aiming at the railroad station plunged ahead. "Whole columns of tanks and motorized infantry were breaking into the center of the city," Chuikov wrote. "The Nazis were now apparently convinced that the fate of Stalingrad was sealed, and they hurried toward the Volga. Our soldiers—snipers, antitank gunners, artillerymen, lying in wait in houses, cellars and firing points—could watch the drunken Nazis jumping off the trucks, playing mouth organs, bellowing and dancing on the pavements."

But now Paulus' soldiers found themselves engaged in a form of warfare they had never experienced. Not even at Leningrad had Hitler permitted his Wehrmacht to fight street by street, building by building—and for good reason. To begin with, the panzers often found their way barred by the debris of the shattered city. Equally important, street fighting canceled out the Germans' superiority in training and teamwork and played into the Russians' raw strength and cunning. Paulus' soldiers were wasted in hand-to-hand combat with ferocious Russians whom one German called in successive diary entries "wild beasts," "not men but devils," and "barbarians," who used "gangster methods."

Whatever they were called, the Russians were enormously skillful in their own unconventional way. Taking advantage of the panzers' tactic of probing for weak spots, the Russians permitted the tanks to penetrate between strong points in abandoned buildings at key intersections, then destroyed them with artillery zeroed in on their path. German infantrymen would rally to knock out the Russian positions, but as soon as one fell, another was quickly established by "storm groups," some of them numbering less than a dozen men. The soldiers in these lethal little units wrapped their feet in padding to deaden the noise of their footfalls and carried shovels with sharpened edges for use both in digging through rubble or in slashing at Germans. Working mostly at night, they stole through alleyways or crept through sewers to seize strategic locations.

One of Paulus' men complained of another Russian ruse: "We would spend the whole day clearing a street, from one end to the other. But at dawn the Russians would start up firing from their old positions at the far end! It took us some time to discover their trick; they had knocked holes between the garrets and attics and in the night they would run back like rats in the rafters, and set their machine guns up behind some topmost window or broken chimney."

Still, the German mass inched forward in central Stalingrad. On the night of September 14 and throughout the next day, heavy fighting raged around Mamayev Hill and Railroad Station No. 1, both of which changed hands several times. Soon after, the Germans drove to within 800 yards of Chuikov's bunker headquarters in Tsaritsa Gorge. He prevented a breakthrough to the Volga only by committing his last reserve of tanks; there were 19 in all. He had to hold the main ferry landing at all costs. Desperately needed reinforcements—10,000 troops of the elite 13th Guards Division—were about to be ferried across from the east bank. If they were prevented from landing, Stalingrad was doomed.

At this point Major S. N. Khopko, commander of a brigade that was blocking the approaches to the landing, hurried into Chuikov's headquarters. According to Chuikov, Khopko reported that he had remaining "one single T-34 still capable of firing, but no longer of moving. The brigade

Cloaked against the chill, Commissar Nikita S. Khrushchev (second from right) surveys an October 1942 battle with the overall commander at Stalingrad, Lieut. General Andrei I. Yeremenko (second from left) and two aides. Khrushchev, the Communist Party's top representative at Stalingrad, held Yeremenko in high regard; at one gloomy point in the fighting, he talked Stalin out of firing the general.

is down to 100 men." Chuikov did not waste time on sympathy. "Rally your men around the tank," he told the major, "and hold the approaches to the port. If you don't hold out, I'll have you shot."

Khopko was killed defending the ferry landing. So were half of his tiny force of survivors. But they held, and boatload by boatload the men of the 13th Guards Division won the race into the Stalingrad caldron. Their commanding officer, Major General Aleksandr Ilyich Rodimtsev, at 36 a veteran of the Spanish Civil War and a Hero of the Soviet Union, was among the first to land; he leaped from his ferry and raced toward Chuikov's headquarters. In his half-mile run, three of his aides were picked off by the Germans.

On Rodimtsev's arrival, Chuikov quickly sketched in the situation. Two of Rodimtsev's infantry regiments were to clear out the center of Stalingrad, and another was to take Mamayev Hill and hold it. Chuikov asked rhetorically if Rodimtsev could do all that. "I am a Communist," Rodimtsev replied. "I have no intention of abandoning the city."

Rodimtsev hurried back to the landing and whipped his units into position as they landed. Slowly, and at great cost, his men made their presence felt. On the morning of September 16, they took Mamayev Hill and dug in for a long fight. But the battle for the railroad station went on day and night, with neither side able to establish firm control. The battle for Stalingrad was becoming an agonizing standoff.

Day after day, scores of savage little fights raged through the central city. One such clash was later recounted by Lieutenant Anton Kuzmich Dragan, whose unit of Rodimtsev's division found itself cut off from the rest of the outfit. "We moved back, occupying one building after another, turning them into strongholds. A soldier would crawl out of an occupied position only when the ground was on fire under him and his clothes were smoldering."

Upon reaching the intersection of Krasnopiterskaya and Komsomolskaya Streets, Dragan and his men took over a three-story building to make a last stand. "At a narrow window of the semibasement we placed the heavy machine gun with our emergency supply of ammunition—the last belt of cartridges. I had decided to use it at the most critical moment. Two groups, six in each, went up to the third floor and the garret. Their job was to break down walls, and

Refugees make way for a German tank on the approaches to Stalingrad.

Two young women, carrying their possessions, emerge from a dugout.

Two women cook their food amid the rubble.

Countless civilians, mostly women and children, camp near the Volga awaiting passage across.

"THERE ARE NO LONGER ANY INHABITANTS"

For the 500,000 civilians who resided in Stalingrad when the German assault began in August 1942, life—as one survivor put it—"was broken off in the middle of a word." In the first two days of bombing alone, 40,000 civilians were killed.

As the Germans blasted their way into the city, a flood of refugees crowded the boats plying the Volga. But German planes and artillery kept the river under constant attack, and the carnage was frightful.

Many Stalingraders chose to stay in their city, to work and fight and die. "Where should I go, away from my factory and my home?" wondered one old worker. In September, workers in Stalingrad's heavily bombed tractor factory turned out 150 armored cars and 200 tanks.

But as the battle reduced the city to rubble, the civilian presence slowly faded. "There are no longer any inhabitants," one observer wrote, "only defenders—rows of sorry lairs in place of the streets."

In the end, when the Germans were at last driven out, only 1,515 civilians came forth from the cellars and other hide-outs. Yet those few meant, as a citizen wrote, that "the city survives in spite of everything. Glory has become our sister amid the ruins of dwellings and the weeping of orphaned children."

Wehrmacht troopers motion for an old peasant woman to leave her underground hiding place.

prepare lumps of stone and beams to throw at the Germans when they came up close."

The German attackers were beaten back, and during the brief lull a German officer shouted through a megaphone: "Russians! Surrender!" Instead, the Russians hoisted a red flag—a vest dyed with the blood of their wounded. "Bark, you dogs!" shouted Dragan's orderly. "We've still got a long time to live!"

"We beat off the next attack with stones," Dragan continued, "firing occasionally and throwing our last grenades. Suddenly from behind a blank wall, from the rear, came the grind of a tank's caterpillar tracks. We had no antitank grenades. All we had left was one antitank rifle with three rounds. I handed this rifle to an antitank man, Berdyshev, and sent him out through the back to fire at the tank point-blank. But before he could get into position he was captured by German submachine gunners. What Berdyshev told the Germans I don't know, but I can guess that he led them up the garden path, because an hour later they started to attack at precisely that point where I had put my machine gun with its emergency belt of cartridges."

Dragan and his men braced for the assault. "This time, reckoning that we had run out of ammunition, they came impudently out of their shelter, standing up and shouting. They came down the street in a column. I put the last belt in the heavy machine gun at the semibasement window and sent the whole of the 250 bullets into the yelling, dirty-gray Nazi mob. I was wounded in the hand but did not let go of the machine gun. The Germans still alive ran for cover in panic. An hour later they led our antitank rifleman on to a heap of ruins and shot him in front of our eyes, for having shown them the way to my machine gun."

The brutal little battle was just about done. "Again," recalled Dragan, "we heard the ominous sound of tanks. From behind a neighboring block, stocky German tanks began to crawl out. This, clearly, was the end." The panzers systematically shelled the building into a pile of rubble, and then departed. But Dragan himself and five others managed to worm their way out of the ruins. They had left behind 32 dead and they had scratched with a dagger on a brick wall the words: "Rodimtsev's guardsmen fought and died for their country here."

After Rodimtsev's 13th Guards Division had been fighting for five days, it finally managed to stabilize the precarious situation, which on the 17th of September had become so desperate that Chuikov was forced to move his headquarters again, this time to a riverside dugout in the factory district. The guardsmen, Chuikov later wrote, "had borne the brunt of the heaviest German blows. They had had to abandon several blocks of houses inside central Stalingrad, but this could not be described as a withdrawal or a retreat. There was nobody left to retreat. Rodimtsev's guardsmen stood firm to the last extremity, and only the heavily wounded crawled away."

While the German drive into central Stalingrad was being halted, Chuikov asked an aide, "What's the situation like on the left wing of the southern city?" In fact, that situation could hardly have been worse. Only one Soviet defensive line remained unbroken, and it was anchored to the huge grain elevator, still filled with wheat. By September 16, a vicious fire fight centered around the elevator.

A German soldier named Wilhelm Hoffmann later wrote, "Our battalion, plus tanks, is attacking the elevator, from which smoke is pouring—the grain in it is burning, the Russians seem to have set light to it themselves. The battalion is suffering heavy losses. There are not more than 60 men left in each company."

Two days later, Hoffmann noted: "Fighting is going on inside the elevator. The Russians inside are condemned men. The battalion commander says, 'The commissars have ordered those men to die in the elevator.' If all the buildings of Stalingrad are defended like this, then none of our soldiers will get back to Germany."

September 20: "The battle for the elevator is still going on. The Russians are firing on all sides. We stay in our cellar; you can't go out into the street. Sergeant Major Nuschke was killed today running across a street. Poor fellow, he's got three children."

September 22: "Russian resistance in the elevator has been broken. Our troops are advancing toward the Volga. We found about 40 Russians dead in the elevator building. Half of them were wearing naval uniforms—sea devils. One prisoner was captured, seriously wounded, who can't speak, or is shamming."

Remarkably, that one prisoner, Andrei Khozyainov, who

Well-armed Siberians of the battle-tested 13th Guards Division take a break in a bunker during the fighting at Stalingrad.

Though Lieut. General Vasily Chuikov received few reinforcements at Stalingrad, the troops he did get were among the Red Army's finest. Many were Siberians, whom a Soviet war correspondent described as being "a sturdy folk, dour, inured to cold and hardship, taciturn, sticklers for order and discipline and blunt of speech. Siberians—they are a rugged folk, men who can be depended upon."

The Soviet High Command was already well acquainted with the Siberians' fighting qualities. In 1941, after the Russians had suffered terrible losses, 34 Siberian divisions—composed of men raised from Siberia's hardy population of "Siberianized" settlers serving on the eastern frontier—were rushed west. The troops had arrived in time to help save Moscow, and later they stiffened the Soviet defenses at Leningrad and Sevastopol. A Russian general said of them, "one such man could, not only morally but technically, be worth 10 or 20 ordinary soldiers."

was a member of a marine infantry brigade, survived to tell the Russian side of the battle for the grain elevator.

"I was called to the battalion comand post," he wrote, "and given the order to take a platoon of machine gunners to the grain elevator and, together with the men already in action there, to hold it come what may. At dawn a German tank carrying a white flag approached from the south. We wondered what could have happened. Two men emerged from the tank, a Nazi officer and an interpreter. Through the interpreter the officer tried to persuade us to surrender to the 'heroic German army,' as defense was useless and we would not be able to hold our position any longer. 'Better to surrender the elevator,' affirmed the German officer. 'If you refuse you will be dealt with without mercy. In an hour's time we will bomb you out of existence.'

" 'What impudence,' we thought, and gave the Nazi lieutenant a brief answer: 'Tell all your Nazis to go to hell!' "

Throughout that day, the beleaguered Russians managed to beat back the German attacks, but conditions inside the grain elevator were becoming worse. Khozyainov recalled, "The grain was on fire, the cooling water in the machine guns evaporated, the wounded were thirsty, but there was no water nearby."

On September 20, a dozen German tanks shelled the elevator. "The explosions were shattering the concrete; the grain was in flames. We could not see one another for dust and smoke, but we cheered one another with shouts. German submachine gunners appeared from behind the tanks. There were about 150 to 200 of them. They attacked very cautiously, throwing grenades in front of them. We were able to catch some of the grenades and throw them back. On the west side of the elevator the Germans managed to enter the building, but we immediately turned our guns on the parts they had occupied. Fighting flared up inside the building. We sensed and heard the enemy soldiers' breath and footsteps, but we could not see them in the smoke. We fired at sounds."

At last the Russians realized they could not hold their position much longer. On the night before the elevator fell, Khozyainov and others attempted to break out—and stumbled onto an enemy mortar battery. "We overturned the three mortars and a truckload of bombs," said Khozyainov. "The Germans scattered, leaving behind seven dead, abandoning not only their weapons, but their bread and water. And we were fainting with thirst. 'Something to drink! Something to drink!' was all we could think about. We drank our fill in the darkness. We then ate the bread we had captured from the Germans and went on. But alas, what then happened to my comrades I don't know, because the next thing I remember was opening my eyes on September

With submachine gun in hand and a food canister on his back, a Red Army soldier (right) clambers over the rubble with rations for Stalingrad's defenders. At far right, cooks make tea in a steaming samovar for the Soviet troops nearby. But tea and even food were sent into the city on a lower priority than vodka, whose power to warm the stomach and steady the nerves was considered vital.

25 or 26. I was in a dark, damp cellar, feeling as though I were covered with some kind of oil. I had no tunic on and no shoe on my right foot. My hands and legs would not obey me at all; my head was singing.

"A door opened, and in the bright sunlight I could see a submachine gunner in a black uniform. I had fallen into the hands of the enemy."

The Russian defense of the elevator had blunted the Fourth Panzer Army's drive in the south. But on September 27, the fighting flared up again in central Stalingrad. Assorted German infantry units of the Sixth Army drove to the top of Mamayev Hill, and the battered defenders—including 2,000 Siberian reinforcements of the 284th Rifle Division— were forced to retreat and dig in on the northeastern slope. Meanwhile, Paulus renewed his offensive in the northern industrial area. After a Stuka bombardment, German units stormed across a Russian minefield, taking heavy casualties but advancing about 2,000 yards. "One more such day," Chuikov later remarked, "and we would have been thrown into the Volga."

At Chuikov's urgent appeal, Yeremenko sent two infantry regiments across the river that night to aid the defenders at the Red October factory. Next day, they were fighting for their lives against another attack. Chuikov said, "The real battle for industrial Stalingrad was only beginning."

Simultaneously, the battle for Mamayev Hill reached a new peak of fury on September 28. At least 500 Germans went to their deaths on the hill that day; the Siberian rifle division alone lost 300 men killed. In both the north and the center, the slaughter continued on September 29.

By October, the generals on both sides were showing physical signs of the unrelenting battle pressure. Paulus had developed a tic in his left eye. He could not stop its twitching, or nail down his near victory. Most of central and southern Stalingrad lay in his hands, but that ruined real estate was worthless to him so long as the northern factory district held out. For what he had won, Paulus had paid a frightful price: 7,700 Germans were dead and another 31,000 were wounded.

Besides worrying about Stalingrad, Paulus fretted over the situation in his rear. In his lunge from the Don to the Volga, he had merely punched a huge hole through the Russian line along the Don. North of his takeoff point, Soviet troops still clung to the Don and even held a bridgehead on the west bank. To pin down these forces, Hitler and Army Group B had been forced to use auxiliary units of Rumanian, Hungarian and Italian troops. Whatever the merits of those allies, Paulus knew full well that they were less than eager to die for Hitler's Germany. Thus the Russian forces on the

Don posed a continuing threat to Paulus' shaky supply line.

For his part, Chuikov was afflicted by a nervous eczema that would henceforth force him to wear bandages to cover the open sores on his hands. If Paulus' losses had been terrible, Chuikov's were ghastly: The Russians had suffered 80,000 casualties and thousands of desertions, among them Chuikov's own deputies for armor, artillery and engineering. In central Stalingrad, Rodimtsev's 13th Guards Division had been so badly chewed up on Mamayev Hill that the survivors had been moved to a relatively quiet sector—the Volga bank around the main ferry landing.

Elsewhere in the city, scores of isolated strong points—tiny Russian islands in the German sea—fought their own private wars. Among these redoubts was a building on Solnechnaya Street, where a handful of men led by a sergeant named Pavlov held out for 58 days; the place became known as Pavlov's House and the sergeant, who survived the War, would always be called the Homeowner.

Chuikov had yet another concern: The weather was unseasonably warm. Although the Russian winter could not be far away and was sure to help his cause eventually, Chuikov knew that the Volga around Stalingrad did not freeze solid quickly; it sometimes took weeks. During that time the river churned with huge slabs of moving ice, rendering it impassable even to armor-sided vessels, and Chuikov dreaded that indeterminate time when the crashing ice floes would cut him off from supplies as well as from reinforcement units that were now arriving from all over Russia.

In any event, Paulus had no choice but to renew his assault on the factory district, just to the south of the line where Hube's 16th Panzer Division had bogged down. On October 2, the Germans opened a long aerial and artillery bombardment, with immediate and dramatic results. Near the Red October ordnance plant stood a huddle of huge oil tanks which Chuikov, in desperate need of fuel, had been mistakenly told were empty. Hit by bombs, the tanks exploded with a blast that shook the devastated city, sending a torrent of flaming oil into the Volga. The burning oil flowed directly over the riverside dugout headquarters from which Chuikov and his staff were trying to control the battle. Officers across the Volga in Yeremenko's headquarters watched the conflagration apprehensively and repeatedly asked Chuikov by radio: "Where are you, where are you?" Finally, Chuikov had time to answer: "We're where the most flames and smoke are."

Two days later, elements of Paulus' infantry and his 14th Panzer Corps tanks launched their attack, moving against the tractor factory, against the Barricades plant, against the Red October works. "It was an uncanny, enervating battle," wrote a German major, "above and below ground, in the ruins, the cellars and the sewers. Tanks clambering over mountains of debris and scrap, crunching through chaotically destroyed workshops, firing at point-blank range into rubble-filled streets and narrow factory courtyards."

In this nightmare world, strange and awful things happened to men's minds. Outside the Barricades factory, a German sergeant named Esser dived for cover behind a wrecked armored car. Glancing around, he saw his company commander nearby—dead. Behind him lay the platoon commander—dead. Just beyond the platoon commander lay a section leader—shot through the head.

Esser went berserk. He jumped to his feet and screamed "Forward!" He dashed across 60 yards of open courtyard—and 12 survivors followed. They reached a factory building, blew a hole in its wall with explosives and then crept inside, coming up behind the Russian defenders who were still

German infantrymen in Stalingrad look skyward as a Luftwaffe attack paves the way for their assault on a Soviet strong point in the autumn of 1942. Although the Luftwaffe attacked constantly, it was subjected to the law of diminishing returns: The more debris it created, the more nooks and crannies the Russians found in which to hide and fight.

firing through windows. Esser and his men scythed down the Russians with their machine pistols. Then they climbed a stone staircase to the second floor of the building. There stood more Russians, slack-jawed with astonishment. Esser took 80 prisoners, captured an antitank gun and 16 heavy machine guns, and left behind scores of Russian dead.

The horror of the fighting also sent a Russian artilleryman named Aleksei Petrov off on a wild killing spree. Petrov had never been in combat before. He had held together well enough even as half of his regiment was killed while crossing the Volga. But then, pressed into service as an infantryman in the northern district, he peered through his field glasses for a comrade who had not returned from patrol— and he spied him. The man was lying face up, pinned to the ground by a bayonet through his stomach.

Shrieking madly, Petrov rushed to a nearby house, followed by some of his comrades. Several Germans tried to surrender. Petrov killed them all with his submachine gun. In a hallway, he heard a German moaning, "Oh God, let me live." Petrov shot the man in the face. Racing from floor to floor, he kicked in doors and killed three more Germans. Then, calm at last, he left the house, now silent.

On October 14, Paulus launched a "final offensive" to smash Chuikov's lines. Three infantry divisions and the tank regiments of two panzer divisions stormed the tractor factory, captured part of it and surrounded the remainder. The Russian defenders continued to fight in scattered groups. In two days of vicious combat at the factory, two Soviet units lost 75 per cent of their men, and soon the bodies of 3,000 German soldiers were mounded up where the men fell in desperate charges into Russian gunfire. In the same period Chuikov evacuated 3,500 wounded men across the Volga.

On October 19, other elements of Paulus' Sixth Army closed in on the Red October and Barricades factories. Half of the Red October plant fell on October 23, but the Russians kept on fighting at the other end, some of them firing from inside the dead foundry ovens. By then the Germans had taken most of the Barricades complex.

Gradually the Germans whittled the Russians down and wiped out their scattered pockets of resistance. Lieutenant Victor Nekrasov, fighting in the Mamayev Hill area, later told journalist Alexander Werth that "toward the end of October, when we had nothing but a few small bridgeheads left on the right bank of the river, the number of troops there was extremely small. Perhaps 20,000 in all."

By early November, Paulus possessed 90 per cent of the utterly desolated city. "Stalingrad is no longer a town," wrote a German officer. "By day it is an enormous cloud of burning, blinding smoke; it is a vast furnace lit by the reflection of the flames. And when night arrives, one of those scorching, howling, bleeding nights, the dogs plunge into the Volga and swim desperately to gain the other bank. The nights of Stalingrad are a terror for them. Animals flee this hell; the hardest stones cannot bear it for long; only men endure." And he added: "My God, why have you forsaken us?"

The ruins were the natural habitat of snipers, and each army had its recognized champions. The Russians in the Lazur chemical works had even set up a school for snipers under the tutelage of Vasily Zaitsev, a onetime shepherd who had perfected his marksmanship while hunting deer in the foothills of the Ural Mountains. In one 10-day period, Zaitsev had killed nearly 40 Germans, and his fame had spread into enemy lines. The Germans retaliated by flying to the scene SS Colonel Heinz Thorwald, the head of their

Constantly on the alert for snipers, two German troopers pick their way through the tangled wreckage of a Stalingrad power plant. While the city was being destroyed block by block and building by building in the protracted fighting, one German bleakly noted in his diary: "Everything in sight is being blotted from the face of the earth."

153

own snipers' school at Zossen, near Berlin. Zaitsev soon heard talk of this deadly new German sniper, and he set down a tense account of their duel to the death:

"The arrival of the Nazi sniper set us a new task: We had to find him, study his habits and methods, and patiently await the moment for one, and only one, well-aimed shot.

"I knew the style of the Nazi snipers by their fire and camouflage. But the character of the head of the school was still a mystery for me. Our day-by-day observations told us nothing definite. It was difficult to decide in which sector he was operating. He presumably altered his position frequently and was looking for me as carefully as I for him.

"Then something happened. My good friend Morozov was killed, and Sheikin wounded, by a rifle with telescopic sights. Morozov and Sheikin were considered experienced snipers; they had often emerged victorious from the most difficult skirmishes with the enemy. Now there was no doubt. They had come up against the Nazi 'super-sniper' I was looking for.

"At dawn I went out with Nikolai Kulikov to the same positions as our comrades had occupied the previous day. Inspecting the enemy's forward positions, I found nothing new. The day was drawing to a close. Then above a German entrenchment unexpectedly appeared a helmet, moving slowly along a trench. Should I shoot? No! It was a trick: The helmet somehow or other moved unevenly and was presumably being held up by someone helping the sniper, while he waited for me to fire.

"A second day passed. Whose nerves would be stronger? Who would outwit whom?

"On the third day, the political instructor, Danilov, also came with us to the ambush. The day dawned as usual: The light increased and minute by minute the enemy's positions could be distinguished more clearly. Battle started close by, shells hissed over us, but, glued to our telescopic sights, we kept our eyes on what was happening ahead of us.

"'There he is! I'll point him out to you!' suddenly said the political instructor, excitedly. He barely, literally for one second, but carelessly, raised himself above the parapet, but that was enough for the German to hit and wound him.

"For a long time I examined the enemy positions, but could not detect his hiding place. To the left was a tank, out of action, and on the right was a pillbox. Where was he? In the tank? No, an experienced sniper would not take up position there. In the pillbox, perhaps? Not there, either—the embrasure was closed. Between the tank and the pillbox, on a stretch of level ground, lay a sheet of iron and a small pile of broken bricks. It had been lying there a long time and we had grown accustomed to its being there. I put myself in the enemy's position and thought—where better for a sniper? One had only to make a firing slit under the sheet of metal, and then creep up to it during the night.

"Yes, he was certainly there, under the sheet of metal in no man's land. I thought I would make sure. I put a mitten on the end of a small plank and raised it. The Nazi fell for it. I carefully let the plank down in the same position as I had raised it and examined the bullet hole. It had gone straight through from the front; that meant that the Nazi was under the sheet of metal.

"'There's our viper!' came the quiet voice of Nikolai Kulikov from his hide-out next to mine.

"Now came the question of luring even a part of his head into my sights. It was useless trying to do this straightaway. Time was needed. But I had been able to study the German's temperament. He was not going to leave the successful position he had found. We were therefore going to have to change our position.

"We worked by night. We were in position by dawn. The Germans were firing on the Volga ferries. It grew light quickly and with daybreak the battle developed with new intensity. But neither the rumble of guns nor the bursting of shells and bombs nor anything else could distract us from the job in hand.

"The sun rose. We had decided to spend the morning waiting, as we might have been given away by the sun on our telescopic sights. After lunch our rifles were in the shade and the sun was shining directly on the German's position. At the edge of the sheet of metal something was glittering: an odd bit of glass—or telescopic sights?

"Kulikov carefully, as only the most experienced can do, began to raise his helmet. The German fired. For a fraction of a second Kulikov rose and screamed. The German believed that he had finally got the Soviet sniper he had been hunting for four days, and half raised his head from beneath the sheet of metal. That was what I had been banking on.

"I took careful aim. The German's head fell back, and the telescopic sights of his rifle lay motionless, glistening in the sun until night fell."

Russian sources credited Vasily Zaitsev with killing 242 Germans before the end of the battle of Stalingrad. Then he was blinded by a detonating land mine.

During the fighting among the factories on October 17, Chuikov had moved again to a safe new headquarters, which his engineers had bored and blasted into the cliff overlooking the Volga. From his vantage point, the general saw a grave danger: Sludge ice was beginning to drift down the Volga, and soon it would form into floes and stop the river traffic. Against that contingency, he had stored away 12 tons of chocolate for his troops. When other supplies stopped crossing the river, Chuikov calculated, he could still hold out for another two weeks by doling out to each man in his army half a bar of chocolate a day.

For the fourth time in the 10 weeks since the battle of Stalingrad started, Paulus' forces had bogged down. But the textbook general was nothing if not stubborn, and he was doubtless inspired by Hitler's latest pronouncement, delivered on November 8 at an anniversary rally in the old Munich Bürgerbräukeller. The Führer had spoken airily of the slaughter at Stalingrad: "I wanted to take it—and you know we are modest—we really have it. There are only a very few small places left there. Now the others say, 'Why don't you make faster progress?' Because I don't want to create a second Verdun but prefer to do the job with small shock troop units."

Those units, then preparing to fly to Stalingrad, were four battalions of fighting engineers, each with 600 men specially trained in demolition of large fortifications. They would spearhead four separate thrusts against different objectives within the factory district.

When the engineers arrived on November 9, they were met by Major Josef Linden, who was to command their operation. Among the targets was the jagged wreckage of the Barricades factory, and Linden appraised it with glum foreboding: "Loosely hanging corrugated steel panels that creaked eerily in the wind—a perfect mess of iron parts, gun barrels, T-beams, huge craters. Cellars were turned into strong points. Over all a never-ceasing crescendo of noise from all types of guns and bombs."

At the Barricades plant, the engineers were ordered to aim their first assaults at two Russian strong points—one of them called the Chemist's Shop and the other known as the Red House. At 3:30 in the morning on November 10, Paulus launched his newest—and, as it would turn out, his last—major offensive.

The Chemist's Shop fell quickly. But the occupants of the Red House fought throughout the day and the following night. Next dawn, when the furious engineers finally burst into the place, the Russian defenders hurried to the cellar. The Germans ripped up the floorboards, tossed down gasoline cans and ignited them with rifle and machine-gun fire. Then they lowered and detonated satchel charges. Now, at last, they were in full possession of the Red House. And there they stayed, trapped by withering fire from other sections of the factory.

Within 48 hours' time, all four of the special offensives mounted by Paulus' engineer battalions had broken down into savage little battles that did not differ at all from the fights that had come before them. Nothing had changed. Scores of clashes ebbed and flowed in the city, day after day, night after night.

On November 14, Chuikov was in desperate straits. In the predawn darkness he sent an angry, despairing message across the ice-choked river: "No ships arrived at all. Deliveries of supplies have fallen through for three days running. Reinforcements have not been ferried across, and our units are feeling the acute shortage of ammunition and rations." Chuikov received no relief. By now he suspected the reason: Something big was up.

At dawn on November 19, Chuikov and Paulus and all their weary men in the ruins heard the boom of big guns from a new direction—far to the northwest. That artillery meant that Paulus' fight to take Stalingrad was over. Those guns meant that a Russian counteroffensive had begun.

AN ARMY OF STREET FIGHTERS

"THEY NEED HELP— THEY ARE WAITING"

One day in the autumn of 1942, about halfway through the five-month battle for Stalingrad, an untested Soviet infantry unit assembled nervously at a ferry slip across the broad Volga from the blazing city. "From this side," a political commissar told the troops, "it looks as though everything is on fire and there's nowhere to set down your feet. But whole regiments and divisions are living there, and fighting well. They need help. They are waiting for you." As each man boarded the ferry, he was handed a leaflet to study on the way across: "What a Soldier Needs to Know and How to Act in City Fighting."

The leaflet detailed the successful tactics developed by Lieut. General Vasily Chuikov, whose battered Sixty-second Army was the backbone of Stalingrad's defense. Chuikov, with never more than 54,000 troops, faced a German Sixth Army that was vastly superior in numbers, training and matériel. But while the enemy came a cropper pursuing rigid tactics of massed assault, Chuikov improvised cleverly and had his men function on their own initiative in small-unit actions, using the city's chaotic ruins as their mainstay. "It would be impossible to enumerate all the new methods our troops worked out," Chuikov wrote. "In the most bitter days of fighting on the Volga we grew, learned, matured— everyone, from the private soldier to the commander."

None of the troops sent across the Volga found much reassurance in the leaflet. Its lessons, learned at such terrible cost, were alarmingly brief. "Get close to the enemy"—this to neutralize the German artillery. "Move on all fours." "Make use of craters for cover." "Dig trenches by night, camouflage them by day."

The new soldiers usually received a terrifying baptism of fire upon disembarking in Stalingrad. "There were times," recalled an observer of the fighting, "when these reinforcements were really pathetic. They would stand there on the shore shivering with cold and fear, 5 or 10 out of 20 already killed by German shells. But the peculiar thing was that those who reached the front line very quickly became wonderfully hardened soldiers. Real *frontoviks*."

Touring Stalingrad's defenses, General Chuikov observes a skirmish nearby. Street fighting, he said, forced each soldier to be "his own general."

Smoke billows skyward from a Stalingrad factory district hit by Stuka dive bombers. The Luftwaffe flew as many as 3,000 sorties a day against the city between August and mid-November of 1942. "By day the enemy's planes hung over our troops, preventing them from raising their heads," wrote Chuikov. "We learned night fighting out of bitter nec...

Since heavy enemy shelling made large-scale assaults suicidal, Chuikov developed small, elusive attack units that fought with submachine guns, grenades, daggers and even sharpened shovels.

These "storm groups" would creep close to their target, wait for the right moment and then charge (left and above). Their tactics, said Chuikov, were the soul of simplicity: "Two of you get into the house—you and a grenade. Grenade first, you after. A grenade in every corner. Then, forward! A burst from your submachine gun around what's left. And get a move on!"

Chuikov expected his troops to turn every house into a fortress. Gutted buildings proved ideal (left and above); there was nothing left to burn, so defenders could not be smoked out. The men seeded the surrounding area with mines and dug long trenches (far left) that enabled them to scurry safely from one building to the next.

Each deadly little maze of strong points created a barrier that was all but indestructible. Protected by interlocking fields of fire, small bands of resolute Russians could —and did—hold off much larger German forces almost indefinitely.

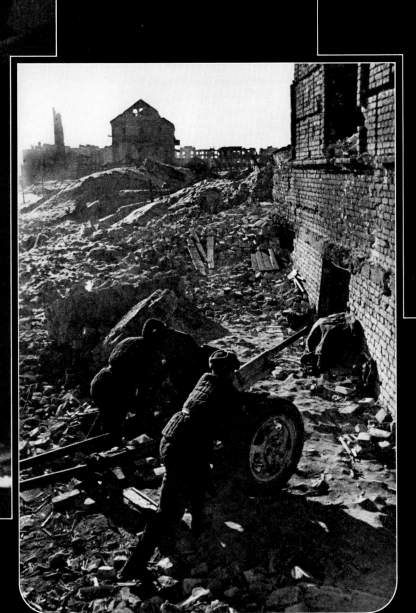

Russians inside a strong point took up positions where their weapons could be used to advantage. Artillery pieces *(left)* guarded open approaches. Submachine guns designed for close-in fighting defended lower floors *(far left)*, and longer-range heavy machine guns and mortars were placed at windows on upper floors *(top)*.

The men held their fire until an enemy unit had advanced into "the killing zone," where gunners could scarcely miss. In one such ambush, two machine gunners in a shattered crossroads house opened fire on an entire German battalion. The two Russians killed scores of enemy troops—and lived to tell the story.

Many small Soviet units mastered the art of killing by stealth. Parties of three to five scouts used the city's deep ravines and rugged Volga banks *(left)* to infiltrate enemy lines; there they would pounce on outposts, slaughter the occupants and flee.

Snipers also hunted in small packs, stealing away at dawn to hidden vantage points *(above and far left)* and drilling any German who showed himself. Sharpshooters accounted for thousands of deaths, and one marksman alone, Nikolai Ilyin *(center, foreground)*, killed 315 Germans.

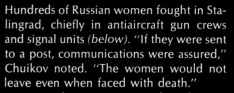

Hundreds of Russian women fought in Stalingrad, chiefly in antiaircraft gun crews and signal units *(below)*. "If they were sent to a post, communications were assured," Chuikov noted. "The women would not leave even when faced with death."

Many other women served as doctors, nurses and combat medics *(left)*. One female medic saved dozens of wounded soldiers by evacuating them from the front alone and without a stretcher. She would wedge herself under a wounded man and, with him on her back, crawl to an aid station, often under enemy fire.

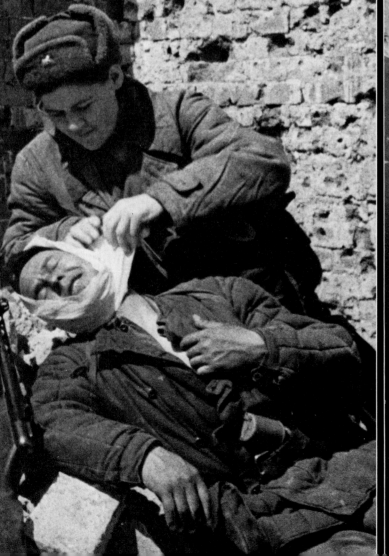

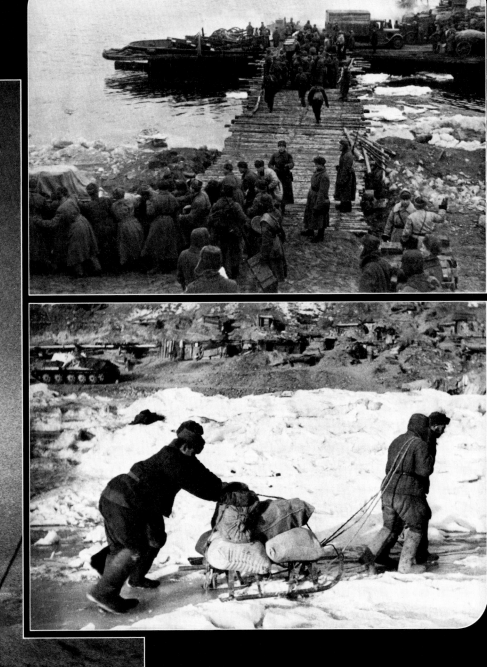

The Russians across the mile-wide Volga from Stalingrad were as resourceful as the city fighters in their efforts to maintain a flow of supplies.

When a ferry carrying ammunition got stuck on a sunken barge, the crew swam to shore, made a log raft and floated their precious cargo to the Stalingrad jetty (inset, top). As soon as thin ice formed on the river, daring soldiers ventured across with laden sleds (inset, bottom). Not until mid-December was the ice thick enough to bear the weight of horse-drawn carts and artillery (left).

Russian improvisation paid off handsomely in late December in the recapture of the Red October steelworks. The troops successfully attacked with small arms and grenades *(left)*. But they needed artillery to break into the last German stronghold, a fortress-like office building. Unable to maneuver a gun through the rubble *(right)*, a storm group brought one into the factory in pieces, then rebuilt it there *(above)*.

"After several rounds at point-blank range," Chuikov recalled, "the Germans ceased to exist."

No Chuikov tactic—no Russian improvisation—altered the battle for Mamayev Hill in central Stalingrad. The savage fighting around the water tanks there *(inset)* raged for 172 days, with the constant bombardment melting several heavy snowfalls. Raw courage alone won the hill—and signaled final victory—on January 26, 1943.

How many times the summit changed hands no one can say," wrote Chuikov in retrospect. "There are no witnesses. They did not survive."

5

The plan for the Soviet counteroffensive was a daring one, and just diabolical enough to strike Stalin's fancy. By that thunderous morning of November 19, it had been in the works for more than two months, and had mustered more men and matériel than any previous battle fought on the Eastern Front. Yet the preparations were carried out so stealthily that until the last minute not even General Chuikov, raging for reinforcements and struggling for survival in Stalingrad's ruins, knew what was happening.

The impetus for the offensive had been provided by Stalin himself on the night of September 12, in a routine meeting with General Zhukov, recently assigned to devise an overall strategy for Stalingrad, and General Vasilevsky, Chief of the Soviet General Staff. At one point, Stalin moved away to study his maps, and the generals discussed, in low, confidential tones, the possibility of saving Stalingrad by means other than a last-man defense. They had not meant Stalin to hear, but the dictator had sharp ears.

"What other way out?" Stalin demanded. Taken aback, Zhukov and Vasilevsky had no ready answer.

"Look," said Stalin, "you better get back to the General Staff and give some thought to what can be done at Stalingrad and how many reserves we will need to reinforce Stalingrad. We will meet again tomorrow evening at nine."

The next night, Zhukov and Vasilevsky arrived with a general concept for an offensive to relieve Stalingrad. But before they could make their presentation, they had to listen to yet another of Stalin's diatribes against his British allies. The British were not sending anywhere near as many first-line fighter planes as Stalin had hoped for. "Tens and hundreds of thousands of Soviet people are giving their lives in the fight against Fascism," Stalin complained, "and Churchill is haggling over 20 Hurricanes. Those Hurricanes aren't even that good. Our pilots don't like them."

Then, with scarcely a break, Stalin asked, "Well, what did you come up with? Who's making the report?"

"Either of us," Vasilevsky replied. "We are of the same opinion." What the generals set forth was far more than a mere attack to break the enemy grip that was strangling Stalingrad. They spoke of a giant pincers movement that would ensnare the entire German Sixth Army. The plan would require ruthlessness, which the Soviet leaders possessed in ample measure, and a delicacy of touch, which

THE TURNING OF THE TIDE

they had never before displayed in the slightest degree.

The offensive would await freezing weather, to give the tanks firm footing, and also the planned November invasion of North Africa by Anglo-American forces, which would pin down German reserves. Meanwhile, Chuikov and his Sixty-second Army in Stalingrad would unknowingly serve as live bait, luring more and more German units into General Paulus' Sixth Army assault on the city. Zhukov would feed in reinforcements stingily, keeping Chuikov just barely strong enough to hold out. As this part of the plan worked out during September and October, the Germans hurled the equivalent of 10 divisions into the attacks on Stalingrad, but only five Soviet infantry divisions crossed the Volga to help in the defense. While giving Chuikov short shrift, Zhukov would patiently gather up all Red Army units as they became available, deploying them on the Germans' northern and southern flanks, opposite the weak and overextended fronts of the Rumanian Third and Fourth Armies respectively. When the time came, the Soviet armies would smash through the Rumanian lines and swing toward a junction at Kalach, on the Don 45 miles due west of Stalingrad, thereby enclosing the German Sixth Army in a fist of steel.

Stalin embraced the scheme. Instructing Zhukov and Vasilevsky to work out the plan in full, he dismissed them that night with a warning: "No one except the three of us is to know about it." And on September 28, on a detailed battle map of the proposed campaign, he affixed the word "Approved" and his signature beneath it. The operation was code-named *Uranus,* after the planet—like Mars and Saturn, symbolic of war.

Zhukov and Vasilevsky obeyed Stalin's demand for secrecy to the letter, refusing even to permit written orders to be drafted. By verbal commands, issued in bits and pieces, a gigantic stockpile of men and matériel began to take form. It came from all parts of the Soviet Union—troops from Siberia, arms from new industries in the Urals, food and more men from the Central Asian republics. The convoys moved by night; the trucks rolled with their headlights out or dimmed, and they took cover during daytime in forests, in ravines, beneath camouflage nets. Troop and supply trains were split into small sections to disguise the size and scope of the movement. In all, more than one million men,

13,451 cannon, 900 tanks and 1,115 aircraft took up their assigned places in the staging areas.

The northern point of attack was to be near Serafimovich, about 75 miles northwest of Kalach, at a point where the Don flows almost due east. There, on the south bank and facing south, the Soviets from the beginning of Paulus' plunge toward Stalingrad had held onto a bridgehead; it was kept under desultory observation by the Rumanian Third Army, which was responsible for a 90-mile front, far more than was warranted by either the Rumanian numbers or their combat skills. To the northwest of the Rumanians stood the Italian Eighth Army and, beyond it, the Hungarian Second Army. The southern attack, set for the second day of the offensive, was to start on a broad front from the southern suburbs of Stalingrad southward against the sector held by the Fourth Panzer and Fourth Rumanian Armies. The Rumanians, who were presumably guarding the right flank of General Hoth's panzers, were especially vulnerable, being stretched thin over an expanse of bleak steppe.

The Rumanians were obvious targets. Out of a sense of national pride, Rumania's Premier Ion Antonescu and Italy's Benito Mussolini had insisted that their armies be autonomous and free of any "corset stiffening" by integrated German units. Hitler had gone along with grave misgivings—for which he had abundant cause.

The Rumanian armies were distressingly primitive in organization, with each division possessing only one antitank company equipped with obsolete 37mm guns. The Rumanians seemed to be more interested in creature comforts than in fighting a war. "The building of defenses," complained a German who had visited the Rumanian lines, "was being neglected in favor of large dugouts for the command posts and shelters for men and animals."

"Papa" Hoth had nothing but contempt for the allies to whom his flank was anchored. He scoffed that "the German commands that have Rumanian troops serving under them must reconcile themselves to the fact that moderately heavy fire, even without an enemy attack, will be enough to cause these troops to fall back, and that the reports they submit are worthless since they never know where their own units are and their estimates of enemy strength are vastly exaggerated."

Despite the Soviet command's best efforts to conceal its

planned offensive, the Germans and the Rumanians could hardly help but detect the enormous build-up. Paulus dutifully passed on the warnings he received. On October 27, he listened with obvious concern to an intelligence summary of the northern sector by Lieutenant Karl Ostarhild, who had painstakingly assembled aerial reconnaissance reports, prisoner interrogations and radio intercepts, and who felt strongly enough about the evidence to present it to Paulus personally. "We have seen a large number of men and matériel concentrated in the region of Kletskaya," Ostarhild stated. "This is an attack army, armed to the teeth, and of considerable size." But Paulus, uncertain of the size of the enemy build-up, issued no alert; he merely distributed a morale-boosting proclamation that advised his units, "It is unlikely that the Russians will fight with the same strength as last winter."

Two days later, Ostarhild's report was confirmed by Rumanian Third Army Commander General Petre Dumitrescu. He told Paulus' superior, General von Weichs of Army Group B, that Soviet troops were crossing the Don in growing numbers and were mounting constant local attacks, "the sole object of which must be to find the soft spots and to pave the way for the major attack." Soon afterward, Paulus brought to army group headquarters a reassuring underestimate of the Russian build-up in the Rumanian sector. "Positively identified," he said, had been "three new infantry divisions with some tanks thought to be concentrated in the area; one new armored, one new motorized and two new infantry formations," and nearby, "two new infantry formations with a few tanks." In fact, the Rumanians were facing the enormous Soviet Fifth Tank Army, consisting of six rifle divisions, two tank corps, a tank brigade, a cavalry corps and assorted artillery and mortar regiments.

Even Hitler, who was not given to overestimating enemy strength, allowed himself a rare expression of anxiety on November 9: "If only this front were held by German formations, I would not lose a moment's sleep over it. But this is different. The Sixth Army really must make an end of this business and take the remaining parts of Stalingrad quickly."

The next day, still vaguely fretful, the Führer ordered the 22nd Panzer Division to drive 150 miles north to support the Rumanians. The results were farcical. The division had been in reserve, its tanks dug in and covered with straw against the increasing cold. Thirty-nine of its 104 tanks would not start, and others dropped out along the way. Mice, it turned out, had been nesting in the straw that blanketed the tanks, and they had nibbled away the rubber insulation of the wiring, causing short circuits. Only 42 tanks were in place behind the Rumanians on November 19—when the roar of guns announced the beginning of the Russian counteroffensive.

The Soviet onslaught was set into motion by a coded radio signal from Moscow: SEND A MESSENGER TO PICK UP FUR GLOVES. At daybreak, 3,500 massed guns began pounding the Rumanian positions. The satellite armies had very little equipment to lose, but hundreds of soldiers died when their bunkers collapsed on top of them. Then, at 8:50 a.m., the Soviet forces attacked from their Serafimovich bridgehead. Hordes of infantrymen plodded forward through the swirling snow and freezing fog, all but invisible in their white winter-combat garb. Later, the ghostly forms of hundreds of Red Army tanks, steering by compass, appeared on a long ridgeline. The Rumanians defended themselves for several hours, but when the Soviet T-34s broke through their line, they were afflicted by what German panzer commander Heinz Guderian called "tank fright." From all sides came the Rumanian cry, "Enemy tanks in the rear!" The Rumanian formations simply dissolved.

German aircraft had no chance to join the battle. "Once again," wrote Luftwaffe commander General von Richthofen disgustedly, "the Russians have made masterly use of the bad weather. Rain, snow and freezing fog are making all Luftwaffe operations on the Don impossible."

By nightfall, a gap 50 miles wide had been ripped in the Rumanian front by the Soviet Fifth Tank and Twenty-first Armies under Major General Nikolai F. Vatutin. As these forces plunged southward, Stalin egged them on with signals that carried a sting. "Tell Zhukov to start more creative operations." "Give Batova push." "Garlinin is too slow."

Next morning came the attack south of Stalingrad—by two fresh armies under General Yeremenko. Still tired and tense after the long ordeal in defense of the city, Yeremenko wanted to wait until the Soviet offensive in the north had drawn enemy reserves in that direction, away from his own front, and he thought it would take more than the day's grace provided in the plan. He had argued the point with the General Staff, but Stavka had rudely rebuffed him. Now, after a sleepless night, Yeremenko dragged his heels past the 8 a.m. starting time, ostensibly waiting for the weather to clear. Stavka impatiently demanded that he get going and finally, at 10 a.m., he began his bombardment. To his considerable astonishment and great gratification, the Rumanians on his front fled in panic, and within a few hours Yeremenko reported that 10,000 prisoners had been taken. By darkness, his Fifty-first and Fifty-seventh Armies had torn open a 30-mile-wide hole and were swinging, in an uppercut arc, northwest toward Kalach.

At that town, an implausible fluke opened the door for the Soviet forces. There stood a crucial bridge across the Don that German truck convoys used to haul supplies to the Sixth Army. It happened that a German training school had been set up at the edge of town and had been using captured Soviet tanks for gunnery demonstrations. Each day the tanks would lumber across the bridge to the west side of the Don, and then when the lessons were over, return to the east bank. The German bridge guards had grown accus-

tomed to the routine, and so, on the morning of November 22, a German sergeant named Wiedemann, having counted off five tanks as they crossed to the west, casually waved on five tanks when they approached to cross eastward. The first three crossed the bridge and fanned out on the east bank. From one of them came a burst of machine-gun fire.

Wiedemann looked more closely. "Those damn tanks are Russian!" he shouted. German 88mm gunfire quickly knocked out the two tanks still on the bridge. But the other three Soviet tanks held the eastern end, under the command of Lieut. Colonel Grigor Filippov. His detachment had been wandering without maps in search of the bridge. Surprised by its easy capture, Filippov radioed for reinforcements, which arrived swiftly. The Germans offered only brief resistance.

Thus the bridge at Kalach was won by the Soviets. The next day, beneath green signal flares that reflected eerily on the snow at a village 30 miles below Kalach, elements of the Soviet Twenty-first Army, which had swept down from the north, joined hands with a tank brigade of the Fifty-first Army, leading Yeremenko's force up from the south. The steel fingers around Paulus' Sixth Army had clamped shut.

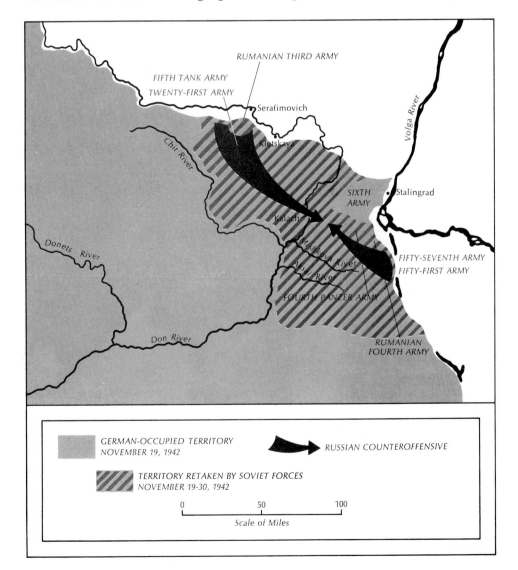

On November 19, 1942, a million Soviet troops launched a two-pronged assault (arrows) to break the siege of Stalingrad. Attacking from the northwest, the Fifth Tank and Twenty-first Armies pushed past the Rumanian Third Army and closed in on Kalach. From the southeast, the Fifty-first and Fifty-seventh Armies punched through the Rumanian Fourth Army and the German Fourth Panzer Army, and then linked up with the northern forces near Kalach. By November 30, the Russians had retaken almost 10,000 square miles (red-striped area) and had squeezed 250,000 Germans into a tiny pocket (gray) west of Stalingrad.

179

Just as easily as that, the first or strategic goal of the Soviet offensive was attained. But the concurrent work of securing the broad belts of land overrun by the converging Soviet spearheads was harder, much harder. It called for the chopping up and grinding down of Rumanian and German troops in the wake of the Red Army's thrusts, and it required Soviet soldiers to die in job lots killing off enemy troops or forcing their surrender. When the bloody business was finished on November 23, the Soviets had killed about 95,000 enemy soldiers, taken 72,000 prisoners, captured or destroyed 4,500 assorted vehicles and liberated 213 localities—all this at a cost of at least 100,000 Russian casualties. And the core of Paulus' Sixth Army had yet to be dealt with.

General Paulus had been having a terrible time of it. On November 20, the day after the Soviet forces rolled off their northern starting line, he and his staff had looked for a potential fall-back defense line along the Chir River, a tributary flowing in a southerly direction across the base of the Don bend. But no sooner had he got there than Hitler, whom he had informed of his plan, radioed him to go back to his headquarters at the Gumrak airfield near Stalingrad and to defend himself there. Paulus and his staff clustered around a clay stove in a 12-foot-square bunker beneath six feet of frozen Russian earth; the only sign of their presence was a curl of smoke that emanated from the snow-covered mound. Paulus planned to draw up his forces south of Stalingrad and set up a hedgehog perimeter—the standard German defense system used so successfully by trapped Wehrmacht units west of Moscow.

Two nights later, foreseeing that the two Soviet pincers would soon join near Kalach, Paulus signaled Army Group B headquarters: "Request freedom of action"—i.e., permission, in case the hedgehog defense failed, to try to break out of the Soviet ring, which was even then about to enclose his army. The plea was relayed to Hitler, who would have none of it, not then, not later, not ever. Back to Paulus came the Führer's command to stay put. "Sixth Army must know," said Hitler, "that I am doing everything to help and to relieve it. I shall issue my orders in good time."

When Adolf Hitler spoke, Friedrich Paulus obeyed; it had always been thus. But by November 23, the Soviet linkup had made Paulus' situation so desperate that he ventured

to beg once again. "The army," he signaled, "is facing annihilation in the immediate future unless the enemy attacking from the south and the west is decisively defeated by the concentration of all available forces. This demands the immediate withdrawal of all divisions from Stalingrad and of strong forces from the northern front. The inescapable consequence must then be a breakthrough toward the southwest."

This anguished appeal drew a reply in the form of a *Führerbefehl* (Führer's Decree)—the highest and sternest of all German commands. "Present Volga front and present northern front to be held at all costs," Hitler ordered. "Supplies coming by air."

By air? The mere idea caused consternation in the German High Command. Lieut. General Martin Fiebig, the Luftwaffe's director of air supplies, first learned of it during a telephone conversation with Paulus' chief of staff, Brigadier General Arthur Schmidt.

"The commander in chief," Schmidt declared, "is thinking of forming a hedgehog defense."

Since an army deployed in this last-ditch defensive posture could make no effort to break out of encirclement, Fiebig asked the natural question: "And how do you propose to keep the army supplied?"

Schmidt replied in his most decisive manner, "That will have to be done from the air."

Fiebig was appalled. "A whole army? It's quite impossible. I advise you not to be so optimistic."

After hanging up on Schmidt, Fiebig immediately protested to his own superior, General von Richthofen, who

Rumanian antiaircraft troops man a frigid sector of the German front west of Stalingrad in December 1942. The Germans were openly contemptuous of their Balkan allies; two Rumanian armies had disintegrated in the face of a Russian counteroffensive in November. Although the Rumanian soldiers were poorly trained and equipped, their greatest handicap was the incompetence and cowardice of their officers, who all too often abandoned their units at the first sign of a heavy Soviet attack.

in turn placed a call to Göring's chief of staff, General Hans Jeschonnek. "You've got to stop it," pleaded Richthofen. "In the filthy weather we have here, there's not a hope of supplying an army of 250,000 men from the air. It's stark-staring madness."

The sorry fact of the matter was that Hitler, at the time he promised to supply Paulus by air, had not even discussed the problem seriously. Not until November 24 did he confer with his top air commanders, including Göring, and with his recently appointed Chief of the General Staff, General Kurt Zeitzler, who was still talking in sensible terms of a Sixth Army breakout. "The Luftwaffe," advised Zeitzler, "should muster every available aircraft and fly in fuel and ammunition only. That way the breakout can succeed."

But Göring, as usual, had in mind a much more flamboyant scheme. "My Führer," he said grandly, "I announce that the Luftwaffe will supply the Sixth Army from the air."

To Zeitzler, the notion was simply preposterous. "The Luftwaffe just can't do it," he said flatly. "Are you aware, Herr Reich Marshal, how many daily sorties the army in Stalingrad will need?"

"Not personally," Göring replied. "But my staff knows."

Zeitzler pointed out that even if all the horses in the encirclement area were slaughtered for food, "it would still leave 500 tons." He angrily repeated the forbidding total: "Every day 500 tons landed from the air."

"I can manage that," proclaimed Göring.

"It's a lie!" shouted Zeitzler.

Hitler intervened. "The Reich Marshal has made his announcement," he said, "and I am obliged to believe him."

The Luftwaffe's effort to supply Paulus by air was a debacle from the start. For one thing, Göring simply did not have enough planes available: only about 180 Ju-52s, fewer than 100 Heinkel-111s and a handful of Ju-86s. Then, too, the pocket occupied by the Sixth Army had only two small airfields, both of them in poor condition. Finally, the Stalingrad zone was then at the edge of a meteorological front where the prevailing weather was foul even for the Soviet Union. During the first 48 hours of the airlift, the Luftwaffe delivered only 130 tons to the Sixth Army, and General Fiebig despairingly noted in his diary: "Weather atrocious. We are trying to fly, but it's impossible. Here at Tatsinskaya one snowstorm succeeds another. Situation is desperate."

As if all that were not bad enough, the Luftwaffe, jealous of its prerogatives, steadfastly refused to let Army quartermasters oversee the supply cargoes. The result was a ludicrous mess. One day, four tons of marjoram and pepper were landed, which at least gave the Sixth Army soldiers something to disguise the taste of the rodents they had been reduced to eating. Then came thousands of right shoes. And, finally, millions of contraceptives.

On December 9, at a time when the Luftwaffe was bringing in an average of 84.4 tons of supplies a day, or less than one fifth the minimal need, two Sixth Army soldiers quietly died of starvation. They were the first of many.

Obviously the Sixth Army would have to look beyond the Luftwaffe for its salvation, and help was already at hand in the form of a man with a magical name and reputation. He was Field Marshal Erich von Manstein, hawk-nosed and with a predatory air, a silver-haired military genius who had ended the interminable siege of Sevastopol by capturing the Crimean fortress within a month of his arrival.

Now, on November 20, Manstein was assigned to command the newly created Army Group Don, comprising Paulus' Sixth Army, the shattered Rumanian Third and Fourth Armies, and most of Hoth's Fourth Panzer Army, which was outside the Soviet ring but still tending its wounds from previous fighting. Of these, the Sixth Army was by far the largest and most powerful, but its nearly 250,000 miserable men—Hitler insisted on calling them "the troops of Fortress Stalingrad"—were huddled within a hedgehog perimeter defending about 450 square miles of open steppe and most of Stalingrad, where they were still locked in battle with General Chuikov's Sixty-second Army.

Soon after receiving his orders, Manstein had a sour foretaste of what was to come. Unable to fly because of blizzards and temperatures of −20° F., he was forced to entrain for his new headquarters. Then he stopped en route to converse with Field Marshal Günther von Kluge, and the commander of Army Group Center gave him fair warning: "You will find it impossible to move any formation larger than a battalion without first referring back to the Führer."

Manstein's orders specified that he was being sent to the Don "for the purpose of stricter coordination of the armies involved in the arduous defensive battles to the south and west of Stalingrad." He was required "to bring the enemy attacks to a standstill and"—given the conditions, the final clause was pure fantasy—"recapture the positions previously occupied by us." But Erich von Manstein was nothing if not a realist: From the outset, he directed his energies toward helping the Sixth Army achieve the breakout that Hitler had expressly forbidden.

Manstein had neither the time nor the troops for anything very sophisticated. He decided to feint from the west toward Kalach, hoping to draw Soviet forces in that direction. Then, in an operation known as *Winter Storm,* he would launch a corps of Hoth's Fourth Panzer Army from Kotelnikovo toward Paulus' perimeter 73 miles to the northeast, and units of the Sixth Army would advance to meet the relief column. The panzer corps would attempt to open and hold a corridor through Soviet lines, permitting food and supplies to be sent in to the Sixth Army. If the panzer corps succeeded, Paulus, upon receiving the radio signal *"Donnerschlag,"* or "Thunderclap," would attempt to break from the Soviet embrace with his whole army. It was a workable plan—if Paulus would fight his way to freedom.

Among the units assigned to the diversion toward Kalach was the 11th Panzer Division, one of several sent from the south to join the drive to rescue Paulus and his army. The division commander was Major General Hermann Balck, a scrawny, stooping, restless man who happened to be one of Hitler's most aggressive tank commanders. Balck's outfit had got itself into trim the tough way—by attrition. "We were fortunate," the general later wrote, "that after the hard fighting in previous campaigns, all commanders whose nerves could not stand the test had been replaced by proven men." The 11th Panzer was probably the best tank division on either side of the front.

By December 7, Balck had raced past Rostov and was approaching the Chir when his column ran full tilt into two Soviet tank brigades heading south. Both sides were surprised but quickly recovered. In and around the sprawling outbuildings of State Farm No. 79, the enemies exchanged gunfire until nightfall. Then the Russians settled into a defensive shell for the night.

Not Balck. Leaving behind him his engineer battalion and a few 88mm guns to put up a show, he swung his tanks west and then north across the snow-covered steppe. Ten hours later, Balck was on the route whence the Russian tanks had come, and he could see a long line of Soviet trucks approaching him, bumper to bumper and filled with infantry reinforcements for the tank brigades he had already encountered. Running parallel to the trucks and firing machine guns so as to save his cannon's armor-piercing ammunition, Balck and his 11th Panzer Division completely destroyed the enemy column.

Then Balck turned south—back toward State Farm No. 79. He caught up with the Russian armor from the rear, just as it was sallying to attack the minuscule formations that Balck had left as his mask. By the end of the ensuing fight, 53 Soviet tanks lay charred and smoking.

Almost immediately, Balck received word that small Soviet bridgeheads were being established along the Chir. Within the last month, the Germans had learned that they could ignore such intrusions at their peril.

In a lengthy preachment on the subject, Balck's parent command, the 48th Panzer Corps, issued a directive declaring, "Bridgeheads in the hands of the Russians are a grave danger indeed. *It is quite wrong not to worry about bridgeheads and to postpone their elimination.* Russian bridgeheads, however small and harmless they may appear, are bound to grow into formidable danger points in a very brief time and soon become insuperable strong points. A Russian bridgehead, occupied by a company in the evening, is sure to be occupied by at least a regiment on the following morning and during the night will become a formidable fortress, well-equipped with heavy weapons and everything necessary to make it almost impregnable. The Russian principle of 'bridgeheads everywhere' constitutes a most serious danger and cannot be overrated. There is again only one sure remedy which must become a principle: If a bridgehead is forming, or an advanced position is being established by the Russians, attack, attack at once, attack strongly. Hesitation will always be fatal."

The 11th Panzer's Balck needed no instruction on the evils of enemy bridgeheads or the virtues of prompt attack. Wheeling westward, he stamped out one bridgehead. Then he moved on to another—but he was too late. Soviet forces from the north had managed to cross the Chir, and nearly 60 of their tanks were waiting for Balck. A pitched battle

German troops hurry to unload a Heinkel-111 bomber ferrying supplies to the surrounded Sixth Army at Stalingrad. The 62-day airlift proved to be a logistical disaster: The Luftwaffe lost some 500 planes and only once managed to deliver the army's minimum daily supply requirements. But the planes did evacuate 35,000 wounded soldiers—and bags of mail that at the end bade farewell to loved ones from those left in the trap.

was exactly what the general wanted least, yet he had it.

Next morning, Balck's tanks attacked, but with the winter sun behind them, several were picked off by Soviet gunners. The fighting went on all day—heavy fighting. Inside the panzers, crewmen were so weary they had to struggle to lift the shells into the cannon breeches. More panzers were knocked out. Others broke down and were abandoned. When night fell, the division had been reduced to half strength and was forced to break off the action.

Facing one such emergency after another, the 11th Panzer Division spent the next two months plugging holes in the German line, fighting mobile defensive battles for which panzers were particularly suited. Yet the division's sacrifice would prove worthwhile if the main body of Hoth's Fourth Panzer Army—and Paulus' Sixth Army—did what was expected of them.

Papa Hoth was ready. At 5:15 a.m. on December 12, his army rolled across the Kotelnikovo starting line to launch Operation *Winter Storm*. In the van was another crack panzer division, the 6th, with its spearhead under the command of a colonel named Hunersdorff. The division was spoiling for a fight. It had suffered through a slow and uneventful journey from distant Brittany, and then the 80 railroad cars on which it traveled had endured constant partisan harassment—torn-up tracks, blown bridges and sniper fire—during its passage across German-held Soviet territory.

On its arrival, the 6th had been assigned to breathe new life into Hoth's combat-weary army, and the panzer division was confident of its strength. As its white-painted tanks crunched northeast through the crusty snow, Colonel Hunersdorff shouted, "Show it to them! Give it to them, boys!"

For two days, Hoth's tanks moved along at a steady pace of about 12 miles a day. Opposition was light but bothersome, with the enemy making full use of the deceptive terrain. Though the steppe seemed level and empty, it was in fact webbed with ravines that were all but concealed by drifted snow. Hidden pockets of Soviet infantrymen emerged from the ravines to harass the German columns. At night, Soviet cavalry rode out to make hit-and-run attacks on the weary German panzer troops in their bivouacs.

On the second day of its march, the attacking panzer division arrived at the 70-foot-wide Aksai River. There it paused to permit 800 trucks carrying supplies for Paulus to catch up. Then the tanks headed toward the Mishkova River, the last remaining natural obstacle on the way to Paulus' pocket.

The lead tanks of the 6th Panzer Division were still 15 miles short of the Mishkova when they ran into the first major formation of Soviet reinforcements, sent to block the threatening movement of the panzer corps. In a swirling fight, the panzers engaged 300 Soviet tanks at ranges of less than a quarter of a mile. German fire discipline proved

superior, and the 6th Panzer left behind 32 flaming T-34s. But as the division inched on toward the Mishkova, the frozen landscape came alive with enemy tanks and infantry, and the lead panzers, exhausted and short of ammunition, clanked to a halt near the village of Verkhne-Kumsky. Within minutes, Hunersdorff drove up in his tank and gave his hesitant troops a dressing down. "Is this what you call attack?" he shouted. "I am ashamed of this day!"

Grimly, the 6th Panzer fired up and moved out, blasting open a corridor, struggling toward the Mishkova. The division got there on December 19, and next morning Hoth informed Manstein that he was in place, ready to launch his final lunge toward the Sixth Army. Now all that remained was for Paulus to begin his part of Operation Winter Storm.

And that was the rub.

Drawn up tight inside his hedgehog, Paulus had put 10 radio operators to work monitoring the progress of Hoth's panzer corps. But the general was in a quandary. Three of his divisions were engaged in heavy defensive fighting in the sector where he was supposed to break out to meet Hoth's panzers; he did not see how he could immediately leap from the defensive to the offensive. Besides, he doubted that his lines would hold until the Thunderclap command authorized his entire army to make a breakout attempt. So Paulus pondered his dilemma and wrote letters. "At the moment," he wrote his wife, "I've got a really difficult problem on my hands, but I hope to solve it soon."

As for Manstein, his communications with Paulus were constantly being jammed by the Russians; however, from the fragmentary exchanges, he got the accurate and alarming impression that Paulus was by no means eager to cooperate with Winter Storm and come out to meet Hoth's panzers. All too clearly, Manstein urgently needed to learn Paulus' intentions, so he sent his intelligence chief, a major named Eismann, to Paulus' headquarters in the pocket. Eismann's little Storch puddle jumper landed at the Gumrak airfield early on December 19, and he was soon in conference with Paulus—and the stubborn General Schmidt.

It was a forlorn mission. Eismann desperately tried to explain that the Sixth Army's only hope lay in a linkup with Hoth. He repeatedly told Paulus that time was running out, that Winter Storm must be launched without delay. Paulus, reported Eismann, hemmed, then hawed about "the magni-

tude of the difficulties and risks that the task outlined to him would imply." Paulus furthermore claimed that his supply shortages made it extremely difficult to wait for Winter Storm to prove itself a success.

Inevitably, Schmidt had his word's worth. He said that even a Sixth Army movement to link up with Hoth's panzers would be "an acknowledgment of disaster"—as if disaster were not already apparent to everyone. Then Schmidt added righteously, "Sixth Army will still be in position at Easter. All you people have to do is supply it better."

His flabby will thus stiffened, Paulus made a strong decision: Winter Storm was "a sheer impossibility"—unless the Thunderclap breakout was authorized simultaneously. Hitler had not yet agreed to Thunderclap. Then, with Eismann gone, Paulus again wrote to his wife. "After the winter," he said, "there is another May to follow."

Paulus' dilemma was a torment to Field Marshal von Manstein as well. He had asked Hitler for permission to give the Thunderclap order, but the Führer had not answered, and Manstein was loath to issue the breakout command on his own authority. Nor could he stand by and wait any longer; a terrible new disaster loomed. On December 16, massive Soviet forces had crashed through the Italian Eighth Army on the upper Don and had begun a giant southerly wheeling movement that threatened Manstein's whole Army Group Don and even imperiled Army Group A in the Caucasus. Manstein knew that right now—with his northwestern flank a shambles, with his strongest army, Paulus' Sixth, surrounded and dying, with his panzer forces extended far beyond the limits of safety—he had to take definitive action.

Thus, on December 23, Manstein ordered Hoth to withdraw from the line of the Mishkova, starting with the 6th Panzer Division, which was already a few miles beyond the river: "The division will be taken out of the bridgehead tonight." As the division departed, one officer stood in his tank turret and saluted to the north—in final farewell to the doomed Sixth Army.

Christmas, dismal and disconsolate, came to the surrounded pocket—and on the holy day 1,280 Sixth Army soldiers died, fewer from wounds than from frostbite, typhus, dysentery and starvation. As a holiday gift to his men, Paulus allowed the slaughtering of 400 horses for food; he could not then bring himself to announce, as he did later that week, that each man's daily ration was being cut to two ounces of bread, one bowl of soup without fat for lunch, and, if it was available, one can of meat for dinner. In the vicinity of a snow-covered wheat field, men waited until darkness, slithered out on their bellies to cut the grain, crawled back to their dugouts and gobbled wheat boiled into soup with water and horse flesh.

There were a few pathetic attempts at celebration. At an outpost designated Hill 135, a tiny pine tree was hung with paper ornaments, and a few candles flickered bravely for nearly an hour—till they were blown out by Soviet mortar shells. To the east, in the besieged ruins of a Stalingrad factory, a single candle, lighted by some unknown mourner, shone over the graves of four German soldiers. From hither and yon across the desolate battlegrounds came voices raised in *"Stille Nacht, heilige Nacht"* and *"O Tannenbaum, O Tannenbaum, wie treu sind deine Blätter."*

On the radio came the voice of Moscow: "Every seven seconds a German soldier dies in Russia. Stalingrad is a mass grave. One . . . two . . . three . . . four . . . five . . . six . . . seven."

During the days that followed, a German soldier—formerly a pianist—wrote in a letter: "My hands are done for, and have been ever since the beginning of December. The little finger of my left hand is missing and—what's even worse—the three middle fingers of my right one are frozen. I can only hold my mug with my thumb and little finger. I'm pretty helpless; only when a man has lost any fingers does he see how much he needs them for the very smallest jobs. The best thing I can do with the little finger is shoot with it."

Another German, one Benno Zieser, wrote with inspired bitterness of the Sixth Army's misery: "The icy winds of those great white wastes that stretched forever beyond us to the east lashed a million crystals of razor-like snow into their unshaven faces, skin now loose-stretched over bone, so utter was the exhaustion, so utter the starvation. It burned the skin to crumpled leather, it lashed tears from the sunken eyes that from overfatigue could scarce be kept open, it penetrated through all uniforms and rags to the very marrow of our bones. And whenever any individual could do no more, when even the onward-driving lash of the fear of death ceased to have meaning, then like an engine which had used its last drop of fuel, the debilitated body ran down and came to a standstill. Soon a kindly shroud of snow covered the object and only the toe of a jackboot or an arm frozen to stone could remind you that what was now an elongated white hummock had quite recently been a human being."

The Sixth Army's suffering did not pass unnoticed by Hitler. On New Year's Day, he sent a radio message to his "troops of Fortress Stalingrad," offering them the thinnest shred of hope: "The men of the Sixth Army have my word that everything is being done to extricate them."

But Hitler had no reason to be hopeful on that New Year's Day. Along the northern half of the battle front, running 600 miles from Leningrad to Orel on the Oka, his armies had been tied up in holding operations for nearly a year. Far to the south, the possibility of future encirclement hung over his Army Group A in the Caucasus; it was vastly overextended. The situation in front of Stalingrad was merely Hitler's most pressing problem.

So far, the Russians had been content to contain the Sixth Army within a steel ring nearly 40 miles deep in places. But that task required the efforts of no fewer than seven Soviet armies, and Stalin needed those armies elsewhere. The time had clearly come to erase the Sixth Army from the battle maps, and the Germans knew it. During the first days of January 1943, German observation posts reported ominous evidence of Soviet build-ups, especially in artillery, along the perimeter of the Stalingrad pocket.

In fact, General Nikolai Nikolayevich Voronov, chief of the Red Army artillery, was in the process of assembling 7,000 guns, more than enough to blast open Paulus' hedgehog. But General Chuikov, still locked with the enemy inside the ruins of Stalingrad, was also to play a key part in the renewed Russian effort.

Chuikov had lately been feeling better about his situation. The pressure on Stalingrad's defenders had of course been eased by the encirclement of the Sixth Army. Beyond that, after a full month in which drifting ice had virtually shut down traffic on the Volga, Chuikov was getting supplies more regularly. Not long ago, in his bunker on the river's west bank, he had heard a thunderous noise. Rushing outside, he had seen a gigantic crest of ice. "Smashing

THE WINTER ORDEAL OF A SHATTERED ARMY

Early on December 16, 1942, the 225,000 men of the Italian Eighth Army awakened to a real-life nightmare along their 60-mile front on the upper Don, northwest of Stalingrad. Troops and tanks of three Soviet armies were charging across the frozen river, heading straight for them. The Italian front collapsed immediately.

Many of the Italians fled—and not unreasonably. They were poorly armed by their own government and held in contempt by their German allies, who allotted them the least and the worst of supplies. They had no tanks and no antitank guns. Their warm-weather shoes offered them no protection from the snow and subzero cold. "Many of the troops threw their shoes away," recalled one Nuto Revelli, [illegible] in rags or blankets."

Within two weeks, the Red Army had advanced more than 90 miles southwest and captured 60,000 Italians. Uncounted others froze to death and were left lying in the snow. Some prisoners managed to escape and were sheltered by Ukrainian families, who gave them more compassion than did their German comrades-in-arms. "The Russian peasant damns the war and the peasant from Sicily damns the war," remarked Revelli. "Their dialogues are simple, essential; they communicate at times with gestures."

The captured Italians were sent on by train to a slow death in Soviet prisoner-of-war camps in the far north. In their [illegible] anything to stay alive. An Italian Army doctor in one camp was horrified to find corpses of prisoners [illegible] they had been cut out.

Perhaps half of the Italian Eighth Army were killed or wounded in the rout on the Don or perished during the brutal winter months that followed. Those who survived—some of whom walked as far as Gomel, about 600 miles to the northwest—crowded onto westbound trains; they were in no shape to fight, so the Germans let them go. By spring, the entire Italian Eighth Army had vanished.

In flight from the advancing Red Army, ragged columns of soldiers from the Italian Eighth Army drag their way west across the treeless Russian steppe.

everything in its path, it crushed and pulverized small and large ice floes alike, and broke logs like matchwood." As Chuikov watched, the great ice wave slowed—and stopped. The Volga was at last frozen solid, and Chuikov's supply ordeal was over since supplies could cross by sled.

Now, to explain Chuikov's role in the new Soviet offensive he commanded, Major General Konstantin Rokossovsky paid a visit to the Volga bunker. During the assaults on Paulus' perimeter, Rokossovsky said, Chuikov's Sixty-second Army must attract more enemy forces in its direction, keeping them heavily engaged. Could Chuikov do the job? Before Chuikov could answer, his aide broke in: "If in the summer and autumn all Paulus' forces were unable to drive us into the Volga, then the hungry and frozen Germans won't even move six steps eastward." As promised, Chuikov's battered little army made work for those German units that chose to fight toward the east.

After talking to Chuikov and before beginning his bombardment, Rokossovsky made an attempt to take the Sixth Army out of action without firing a shot. On January 8, a Soviet captain bearing a white flag appeared at a German position on the western nose of Paulus' hedgehog and handed the local commander a letter offering surrender terms. News of the offer crackled throughout the Sixth Army and, even before the document reached him, Paulus sent out orders forbidding anyone to enter into surrender negotiations of any sort. When he did receive the letter, Paulus flatly turned it down and suppressed the contents.

Next day the Russians showered the entire Sixth Army defense zone with air-dropped leaflets giving their terms along with the warning that "anyone resisting will be mercilessly wiped out." The wretched German troops must have thought the surrender offer more than generous:

"We guarantee the safety of all officers and men who cease to resist, and their return at the end of the war to Germany or to any other country to which these prisoners of war may wish to go.

"All personnel of units which surrender may retain their military uniforms, badges of rank, decorations, personal belongings and valuables and, in the case of high-ranking officers, their swords.

"All officers, noncommissioned officers and men who lay down their arms will immediately be given normal rations.

"All those who are wounded, sick or frostbitten will be given medical treatment.

"Your reply is to be given in writing by 3 p.m., Moscow time, 9 January, 1943."

The appeal for Paulus' surrender was useless; he would obey his Führer. In so doing, he would pin down Soviet forces that would otherwise be used against the German armies in the Caucasus. And then on the morning of January 10, the day after the ultimatum ran out, Voronov's guns began to boom.

Above the barrage swarmed Soviet planes, and surging through deep snow, came tides of tanks and infantry, red flags flapping. Huge holes in the German lines were almost instantly ripped open. But the German forces closed the gaps and doggedly fought a controlled retreat, maintaining a solid perimeter for nearly a week.

In the west, the Austrian 44th Division held on gallantly. One of its battalions, defending the approaches to the airstrip at Pitomnik, was under the command of a major named Pohl, who had recently received from Paulus a Knight's Cross, accompanied by a more useful reward: a loaf of bread and a can of herring in tomato sauce. Pohl was determined to hold the line at all costs, and so was the sergeant in charge of the battalion's last heavy machine gun, who had told Pohl, "No one's going to shift me from here, Herr Major." But suddenly Pohl saw Soviet soldiers leaping into the firing pits; the sergeant was killed and Pohl joined the retreat. By January 22, the Austrians, along with the rest of the Sixth Army, were fleeing headlong into the city of Stalingrad. There they joined German units that were battling Chuikov's troops.

Just outside the city at the Gumrak airfield, Paulus was still insisting that the Luftwaffe supply his army even though the wreckage of 13 planes scattered across the runways supported the Luftwaffe's contention that Gumrak was no longer operable. Paulus was in a pitiable state; the tic that had afflicted one eye now extended from brow to jaw. A Luftwaffe liaison officer bore the brunt of Paulus' despair. "If your aircraft cannot land, my army is doomed," Paulus shouted. "It is four days since they have had anything to eat. The last horses have been eaten up."

One of Paulus' officers joined in. "Can you imagine," he asked the hapless Luftwaffe man, "what it is like to see soldiers fall on an old carcass, beat open the head and swallow the brains raw?"

Paulus continued, "What should I, as the commander in chief of an army, say when a simple soldier comes up to me and begs, 'Herr General, can you spare me one piece of bread'?" Paulus could not stop. "Why on earth did the Luftwaffe ever promise to keep us supplied? Who is the man responsible for declaring that it was possible? Had someone told me it was not possible, I should not have held it against the Luftwaffe. I could have broken out. When I was strong enough to do so. Now it is too late."

It was indeed. Gumrak fell to the Russians, who soon drove Paulus back to the place where his troubles began: Stalingrad. He moved into a new headquarters in a basement warehouse beneath the shell of the Univermag Department Store on Red Square. There he shared with his troops the onslaught of an old enemy, Chuikov, and a new one: hordes of lice that covered the emaciated bodies of the German men with angry red welts.

Completely convinced that the Sixth Army's agony was in vain, Field Marshal von Manstein pleaded with Hitler to permit Paulus to surrender. His efforts were wasted. Hitler would not face up to the facts. Instead, he cast about for miracles and found absurdities. On January 23, in a meeting with several high-ranking officers at the Wolf's Lair, the Führer discussed in dead earnest an irrational scheme for forming a battalion of new Panther tanks and using it to carry supplies through enemy lines to Paulus' perimeter.

"I was flabbergasted," said Major Coelestin von Zitzewitz, Hitler's liaison officer with the Sixth Army in Stalingrad. "A single panzer battalion was to launch a successful attack across several hundred miles of strongly held enemy territory when an entire panzer army had been unable to do so. I used the first pause that Hitler made in his presentation to describe the hardships of the Sixth Army; I quoted examples, I read off figures from a slip of paper I had prepared. I spoke about the hunger, the frostbite, the inadequate supplies, the sense of having been written off; I spoke of wounded men and lack of medical supplies.

"I concluded with the words: 'My Führer, permit me to state that the troops at Stalingrad can no longer be ordered to fight to their last round because they are no longer

Smartly decked out in new uniforms complete with epaulets denoting rank, a Russian major general (right) and two of his aides map out tactics at a divisional headquarters near Stalingrad in 1943. The shoulder boards symbolized the enhanced prestige and professionalism of the Red Army officer corps following the decisive Russian victory at Stalingrad.

physically capable of fighting and because they no longer have a last round.'

"Hitler regarded me with surprise, but I felt he was looking straight through me. Then he said: 'Man recovers very quickly.' With these words I was dismissed."

Hitler's final response to Zitzewitz' argument was to send a radio message to Stalingrad: "Surrender out of the question. Troops will resist to the end."

Next day in Stalingrad a German general officer, depressed by news of his son's death in combat and unwilling to face Siberian captivity, put a pistol to his head and pulled the trigger. Another general, named Hartmann, commander of the skeletonized 71st Infantry Division, put down the book he was reading and observed to a fellow officer: "As seen from Sirius, Goethe's works will be mere dust in a thousand years' time, and the Sixth Army an illegible name, incomprehensible to all." With that, Hartmann went outside, rounded up a small group of men and led them to a railway embankment. There, standing upright and deliberately exposing himself to the enemy, he shouted, "Commence firing!" He blazed away with his rifle until the Russians cut him down.

On that same day, Sixth Army headquarters sent Manstein a signal that quivered with pain: "Frightful conditions in the city area proper, where about 20,000 unattended wounded are seeking shelter among the ruins. With them are about the same number of starved and frostbitten men, and stragglers, mostly without weapons, which they lost during the fighting. Heavy artillery is pounding the whole city area."

Hitler's reaction: "Surrender is forbidden. Sixth Army will hold their positions to the last man and the last round, and by their heroic endurance will make an unforgettable contribution towards the establishment of a defensive front and the salvation of the Western world."

This was the end.

On January 30, Hitler notified Paulus that he had been made a field marshal. The dictator's motive was both macabre and transparent: Never before, in any war, had a German field marshal surrendered his command, and Hitler hoped that Paulus would measure up to that proud tradition—either by dying in battle at the head of his men or by committing suicide. To Friedrich Paulus, the textbook soldier, the second alternative was unthinkable; days before, he had issued an order denouncing suicide as a "disciplinary infraction."

At 5:45 a.m. on January 31, 1943, an operator at Sixth Army headquarters sent a final message:

"The Russians stand at the door of our bunker. We are destroying our equipment.

"This station will no longer transmit."

Minutes later, a young Soviet tank lieutenant named Fyodor Yelchenko entered the headquarters in the Univermag basement with two other soldiers. From a side room, Paulus stepped out to meet the lieutenant. "Well," said Yelchenko, "that finishes it."

Paulus and his chief of staff Schmidt were placed in a

Soviet staff car and driven south past landmarks that had come to have a grisly renown: the Tsaritsa Gorge, the grain elevator, the ruins of Dar Gova. And at a farmhouse in the suburb of Beketovka, Paulus identified himself to General Shumilov, commander of the Sixty-fourth Army.

A few days after surrendering, Paulus, along with his staff, was taken from the building for public display. Reported a Soviet war correspondent: "We weren't allowed to speak to him; he was only shown to us. (We could then testify that he was alive and had not committed suicide.) He gave us a look, then stared at the horizon, and stood on the steps for a minute or two, amid a rather awkward silence, together with two other officers; one was General Schmidt, his chief of staff, a sinister creature, wearing a strange fur cap made of imitation leopard skin. Paulus looked pale and sick. He had more natural dignity than any of the others, and wore only one or two decorations."

Paulus' surrender was shocking news to Hitler, and he took it with rambling rage. Why had Paulus failed to kill himself? That dark thought filled a transcript of his subsequent staff conference with General Zeitzler and others:

Hitler: When you consider that a woman has the pride to leave, to lock herself in, and to shoot herself right away just because she has heard a few insulting remarks, then I can't have any respect for a soldier who is afraid of that and prefers to go into captivity.

Zeitzler: I can't understand it either. I'm still of the opinion that it might not be true.

Hitler: No, it is true. A man who doesn't have the courage in such a time to take the road that every man has to take at some time doesn't have the strength to withstand that sort of thing. He will suffer torture in his soul. In Germany there has been too much emphasis on training the intellect and not enough on strength of character.

Zeitzler: There is no excuse. When his nerves threaten to break down, then he must kill himself.

Hitler: When the nerves break down, there is nothing but to admit one can't handle the situation, and to shoot oneself. One can also say that the man should have shot himself just as the old commanders who threw themselves on their swords when they saw that their cause was lost. That goes without saying. When the Roman Varus was defeated in Germany, he gave his slave the order: "Now kill me."

Zeitzler: I still think they may have done that and that the Russians are only claiming to have captured them all.

Hitler: No. In this war no more field marshals will be made. This hurts me so much because the heroism of so many soldiers is nullified by one single characterless weakling—and that is what the man is going to do now. You have to imagine, he'll be brought to Moscow, and imagine that rattrap there. There he will sign anything. He'll make confessions, make proclamations—you'll see."

In spite of Hitler's abuse, Paulus had lived up to his Führer's trust in at least one sense: He had surrendered only himself and his staff—and not the Sixth Army. The army was free to fight on—if it would and could. But it could not and did not.

Left to itself amid the ruins it had created, that army during the next 48 hours threw down its arms and raised its hands. The army surrendered in ones and twos, in isolated groups and in larger units—all of the men once proud but now broken by defeat, injury and famine. A sick, exhausted German soldier, when asked why he surrendered instead of killing himself, replied, "You have to be in good form to commit suicide."

Three days later, on February 3, a lone Luftwaffe Heinkel-111 flew low over the snow-covered, fog-shrouded steppe between the Volga and the Don, seeking out Sixth Army survivors to whom it might drop supplies. Finally, the pilot looked to his radio operator, who shook his head and said: "Nothing anywhere."

No one will ever know the full cost of Stalingrad. Ninety-nine per cent of the city lay in ashes; 41,000 homes, 300 factories, 113 hospitals and schools.

The human casualties—dead, wounded, missing and taken prisoner—could only be estimated: 300,000 Germans, 200,000 Rumanians, 130,000 Italians, 120,000 Hungarians. The Soviet forces had lost something like 750,000 men.

The victory at Stalingrad—the rock-hard defense inside the city and the sweeping offensive that engirdled it—brought forth a Red Army far different from the one that had wallowed in the mire of defeat through the summer of 1942. During that dreadful period, Stalin, perhaps more in wishfulness than in belief, had forecast to Winston Churchill the transformation of his forces, saying, "They are not so hot yet, but they are learning, and they'll make a first-class army before long." Awful though it was, Stalingrad had been a classroom beyond compare.

In the caldron, a rabble in arms had become an army in spirit, in tactics, in strategy, in command. General Rodion Yakovlevich Malinovsky, whose troops had helped turn back Manstein's Operation *Winter Storm,* said, "Our men have far greater experience. And they can now face situations that they could not face a year ago—for example an onslaught by 150 tanks." In early December, more than six weeks before Paulus' surrender, United Press correspondent Henry Shapiro had visited the Soviet troops mopping up the Serafimovich battlefield, and he reported, "I found among the officers and soldiers an air of confidence the like of which I had never seen in the Red Army before." An editorial in *Red Star* boasted, "Today we are like iron, like steel, like a steel spring ready to shoot out and strike the enemy with double or treble force."

Some of the changes in the Red Army were cosmetic, or so it seemed. Stalingrad had returned to the soldiers those symbols that had forever rallied fighting men. For the first time since Russian soldiers in 1917 ripped the emblems of rank off their officers' shoulders, shoulder boards with colored stripes were authorized for enlisted men, and gold and silver braided epaulets went to officers. (The consequent Soviet request for 30,000 yards of gold and silver braid caused British aid authorities to shake their heads in annoyance.) The Red Army now demanded military respect and respected military protocol. Soldiers were required to salute their officers, who in turn were forbidden to demean themselves by such plebeian practices as carrying large parcels through the streets or wearing *valenki* (felt boots) to the theater. And high-ranking officers could not ride on public transportation. However, an editorial in *Red Star* hastened to explain that "the attention given to the officer's and soldier's bearing and outward appearance cannot be regarded as nonrevolutionary."

New banners were issued to Red Army units amid pomp and circumstance worthy of Napoleon's Old Guard. As *Red Star* described the ritual, "After the congratulatory speech by the representative of the People's Commissariat of Defense, the commanding officer, kneeling, together with all his men, himself kisses the banner three times; then, rising to his feet, he reads the oath on behalf of the unit. Then the men also rise. The commanding officer then hands the banner to the banner bearer. The band then plays the 'Internationale.'"

Spiritually uplifting though these moves may have been, they would have been useless had it not been for a revolution in the Soviet command. Gone from the Army, or temporarily sidelined, were such old Stalin drinking companions as Voroshilov and Budenny, such habitual losers as Timoshenko and such timorous lesser leaders as Lopatin. The men who replaced them had been carefully picked for Stalingrad because their performances earlier in the War had shone like diamonds in dung; they had saved the city on the Volga and now they were eager to carry the war to the Germans. In the event, Yeremenko would liberate the Crimea and Sevastopol, while Chuikov would one day receive the German surrender at Berlin. During and shortly after Stalingrad, Zhukov and Vasilevsky were named marshals, and within two years three more graduates of Stalingrad would attain the same exalted rank: F. I. Tolbukhin, Konstantin Rokossovsky and Rodion Malinovsky.

Tactically, the new Soviet breed borrowed liberally from the German invaders. Artillery and armor were taken from smaller units and massed in divisions and corps; artillery and air forces cooperated closely with ground troops in

Haggard and unshaven, the German Sixth Army commander, Friedrich Paulus (left), leads two of his staff officers as they are taken into captivity on January 31, 1943, at the Russian Sixty-fourth Army headquarters.

blasting open breaches in enemy lines for deep penetration by tanks. In terms of strategy, even Moscow's armchair experts knew what had to be done. "The keynote in the education of our Red Army," advised *Red Star*, "now must be that defense can be considered only as something temporary—without decisive offensive operations the enemy can never be smashed."

Easily said. But to change nearly 12 million men, spread over the world's largest nation, from a strategic defense that had lasted more than a year to a war of offense was an undertaking of difficulty almost beyond human comprehension. It did not happen immediately. The Russians still had much to learn about mobile warfare—and Germans like Manstein would administer some bitter lessons during the next few months. But the change began at once.

The Red Army's path now lay in a new direction. Alexander Werth, the London *Sunday Times* correspondent, followed that path.

"All the forces in Stalingrad were now being moved— towards Rostov and the Donets," wrote Werth shortly after the battle. "About midnight we got stuck in a traffic jam. And what a spectacle that road presented—if one could still call it a road! Weird-looking figures were regulating the traffic—soldiers in long white camouflage cloaks and pointed white hoods; horses, horses and still more horses, blowing steam and with ice round their nostrils, were wading through the deep snow, pulling guns and gun carriages and large covered wagons; and hundreds of lorries with their headlights full on. To the side of the road an enormous bonfire was burning, filling the air with clouds of black smoke that ate into your eyes; and shadow-like figures danced round the bonfire warming themselves; then others would light a plank at the bonfire, and start a little bonfire of their own, till the whole edge of the road was a series of small bonfires.

"Such was the endless procession coming out of Stalingrad; lorries, and horse sleighs and guns, and covered wag-

ons, and even camels pulling sleighs—several of them stepping sedately through the deep snow as though it were sand. Every conceivable means of transport was being used. Thousands of soldiers were marching, or rather walking in large irregular crowds, to the west, through this cold deadly night. But they were cheerful and strangely happy, and they kept shouting about Stalingrad and the job they had done.

"Westward, westward! How many, one wondered, would reach the end of the road? But they knew that the *direction* was the right one. In their felt boots, and padded jackets, and fur caps with the earflaps hanging down, carrying submachine guns, with watering eyes, and hoarfrost on their lips, they were going west. How much better it felt than going east!"

These immense rambling Soviet forces were headed for the Caucasus, where German Army Group A under General von Kleist had stuck its head in a noose. In August 1942, even as Paulus began his advance on Stalingrad as the northern prong of Operation *Blau,* Kleist and his southern prong had driven eastward in what at first amounted to little more than a pleasant drive through the Caucasian countryside. By the end of August, Kleist had arrived some 450 miles east of Rostov—and there, pinched by the Caucasus Mountains and confronted by a crossing of the Terek River, Army Group A was unexpectedly brought up short by fuel shortages, complicated by defense works that had been frenziedly thrown up by the region's civilian population.

"People worked until they nearly collapsed," wrote the Soviet trans-Caucasian front commander, General I. V. Tyulenev, "with bloody rags round their blistered hands. By the beginning of autumn about 100,000 defense works were built, including 70,000 pillboxes and other firing points. More than 500 miles of antitank ditches were dug, 200 miles of anti-infantry obstacles were built, as well as 1,000 miles of trenches. Something like nine million working days were expended on this work."

By January, with Paulus encircled at Stalingrad, the Soviet

Promoted during and just after Stalingrad, Aleksandr Vasilevsky (far left) and Georgy Zhukov appear in the bemedaled and braided uniforms of Marshals of the Soviet Union. The generals were elevated to the Red Army's highest rank in recognition of their roles as chief architects of the stunning Soviet victory.

generals were ready to tighten the noose on Kleist. In perhaps their major strategic offensive so far, they attempted to slash through Kleist's left flank at Elista; in another movement, they attacked northward toward Armavir, from the Terek River and through the Caucasus passes. In a third operation, most dangerous of all to the Germans, the forces of Vatutin and Yeremenko drove down the Don toward Rostov, the bottleneck to the Caucasus through which all of Kleist's supplies must pass.

Kleist found himself in a desperate predicament. "When the Russians were only 40 miles from Rostov and my armies were 390 miles east of Rostov," he wrote later, "Hitler sent me an order that I was not to withdraw under any circumstances. That looked like a sentence of doom. On the next day, however, I received a fresh order—to retreat, and bring away everything with me in the way of equipment."

He did not waste time making ready to depart; he left at once and, almost miraculously, he made it, the Russian spearheads closing just behind him as he went. On February 14, 1943, Rostov fell to the Soviet armies, but not before the last units of Army Group A had passed through to safety. For his masterly performance, Kleist was made a field marshal—surely the first time Hitler had promoted one of his generals for presiding over a retreat. This was an ominous sign of the change in German fortunes.

In fact, the Soviet strategic concept had by far outstripped the supply facilities and administrative skills necessary to carry it out. Among other things, the generals had launched their offensive with less than half the transport needed to bring up food, fuel and ammunition—a case of rampant optimism based on the remarkable assumption that they could make up the shortages with captured German supplies. It worked for a while, but as the Soviet lines lengthened, and as Kleist proved to be most miserly about giving up his necessaries, the Soviet drives slowed. Kleist had thus escaped. Yet though the Red Army had failed to bag the enemy, it had succeeded in clearing the vital Caucasus—for good.

Meanwhile, far to the north, the Russians burst through thin German lines, took Kursk on February 8 and created a gigantic salient that bulged westward into the German lines. The Germans had used Kursk as a springboard for their summer offensive against Stalingrad in 1942; the Soviet forces hoped to use it as a launching platform for a drive to the north against Orel. The salient posed a threat that the Germans could not afford to ignore.

The capture of Kursk was overshadowed on February 16 by the Soviet seizure of Russia's fourth largest city—Kharkov. Lime trees and poplars still graced the avenues, but Kharkov had otherwise suffered terribly in German hands. Its prewar population of about 900,000 had been reduced by two thirds: Uncounted thousands had fled; an estimated 120,000 citizens, mostly young people, had been deported to German labor camps; some 70,000 to 80,000 had died of hunger and cold; and perhaps 30,000, including 16,000 Jews, had been slaughtered by the Germans. Stalin celebrated the recapture of Kharkov by naming himself a Marshal of the Soviet Union and proclaiming: "The mass expulsion of the enemy from the Soviet Union has begun."

Not quite yet. On the 15th of March, 1943, the Germans recaptured Kharkov, storming into one hospital and brutally killing 200 wounded before setting it afire. Early thaws and heavy spring rains then turned the entire Russian front into a morass, and an eerie three-month lull fell upon the far-flung battlefields. Both sides used the breathing spell to plan feverishly for their 1943 summer campaigns—and the Germans focused their attention on that huge Soviet salient around Kursk.

At Kursk in July would be fought the biggest tank battle in history, a milling, brawling, murderous battle that probably did more than any other to decide the outcome of the war on the Russian front. Though the fighting would last two more years, the road from Stalingrad would lead inexorably toward Berlin for a Red Army no longer merely resurgent—but victorious.

A NEW PRIDE AND SPIRIT

On the verge of victory, Stalingrad's defenders joyfully embrace comrades of the Twenty-first Army, which chopped through German lines on January 26, 1943.

"LIKE A MEDAL ON THE CHEST OF EARTH"

Three paraders typify the many contributors to victory: a Red Army soldier (left), a civil-war veteran and a marine, detached from the Caspian Fleet.

After 163 days of almost constant gunfire, the last shot was fired at Stalingrad on February 2, 1943. In the strange and lengthening silence, the survivors of the battle realized slowly that the fighting would not begin again. Only now could they safely claim what was theirs at Stalingrad.

They and their comrades in the resurgent Red Army had dealt a crushing defeat to the Third Reich. The battle had cost Hitler most of five armies—nearly a quarter of his soldiers on the Russian front—and an arsenal of equipment that would take half a year to replace. "Never before in Germany's history," wrote General Siegfried Westphal, "had so large a body of troops come to so dreadful an end."

Defeat was chiseled into the faces of more than 91,000 captured German soldiers—emaciated, threadbare figures shuffling to collection points for registration and screening. "Scarecrows" was what Sergeant Ivan Bratchenko, a Soviet artilleryman, called the prisoners. "Their heads were wrapped in torn blankets and rags. Some had tied sacks or shreds of overcoats to their boots; others had stuffed their feet into enormous straw overshoes. Many were wounded or frostbitten. Worn-out, unshaven, with soot and dirt on their faces, they wore a tortured expression, as if they just had been taken down from a cross."

The Russians had won their first strategic offensive of the War. The men who had so long defended the ruins of Stalingrad celebrated on the evening of February 2 with the troops that had engulfed the German attackers. The victors fired thousands of German signal flares, splashing multicolored fireworks across the sky. Two days later they held a mass rally in a plaza aptly named the Square of the Fallen Warriors. Then the troops left Stalingrad and headed for new battles elsewhere.

But Stalingrad never left the Red Army. The battle there had given every Soviet soldier a tradition of victory, a reason for confidence, pride and *esprit de corps*. "This city is like a medal on the chest of the earth," wrote Bratchenko. "On the soul of every defender it has left a trace like the annual ring on the trunk of a tree."

A lengthy column of German prisoners snakes across the snowy steppe toward temporary prison camps near Stalingrad. Some columns marched unguarded.

At a mass awards ceremony, Soviet General Kuzma Gurov pins the Order of the Red Banner, for military excellence, on a colonel who helped take Mamayev Hill.

The rewards of victory were bountiful at Stalingrad. Every one of the 707,000 Russians who took part in the battle received a medal. Nearly all of the units earned the honorific title Guards. More than 100 men received the greatest honor of all: to be designated a Hero of the Soviet Union.

For the Red Army, there were mountains of matériel to turn against the enemy who had brought it. Stalingrad and its suburbs were clogged with so much weaponry and equipment that the Russians spent weeks collecting it. All in all, the Soviet forces claimed to have seized 750 planes, 1,550 tanks, 61,000 trucks, 56 locomotives, 1,125 railway cars, 6,700 heavy guns, 1,462 mortars and nearly 100,000 small arms.

The Germans who were captured faced a harsh future—but not uniformly harsh. The 24 generals taken at Stalingrad were disarmed and interrogated. (In a nervous jest, Lieut. General Walther von Seydlitz-Kurzbach—shown at right—offered to surrender his penknife, and was told to keep it.) After a few days, most of them were sent to the outskirts of Moscow, where they spent their time in a comfortable cluster of fenced-in summer cottages.

But the great mass of prisoners did not fare so well. Half of them died of typhus in temporary POW camps near Stalingrad, and thousands more perished in permanent camps in Central Asia.

BOUNTIFUL REWARDS FOR AN ARMY OF VICTORS

Grinning Russian youngsters strut around a farming village carrying
a heavy load of German trophies—ammunition belts, machine guns and
rifles they have gathered in the battlefields outside Stalingrad.

Six captured German commanders glumly await interrogation at Sixty-second Army headquarters in Stalingrad. General von Seydlitz sits third from the right.

German helmets by the thousands await salvage for their steel. More personal relics of the German soldiers littered their former camps: books, maps, letters to their families and snapshots of their loved ones.

Corpses lie in mounds on a frozen field outside Stalingrad. Many of the dead were stripped of their trousers and boots; then the bodies were burned on giant pyres constructed of railroad ties. "I once went out to watch," said Nikita Khrushchev, "but I didn't go back a second time."

Victorious Russians sing and dance in a Stalingrad square lined with gutted buildings. The music was crude, but it sounded sweet—on liberated accordions.

BIBLIOGRAPHY

Alexander, Jean, *Russian Aircraft since 1940*. London: Putnam & Company, 1975.

Armstrong, John A., ed., *Soviet Partisans in World War II*. University of Wisconsin Press, 1964.

Baldwin, Hanson, *Battles Lost and Won: Great Campaigns of World War II*. Harper & Row, 1966.

Barna, Yon, *Eisenstein*. Little, Brown, 1975.

Batchelor, John, and Ian Hogg, *Artillery*. Charles Scribner's, 1972.

Biryukov, G., and G. Melnikov, *Antitank Warfare*. Progress Publishers, no date.

Bratchenko, Ivan, *Ogon vedut katyushi*. Dnepropetrovsk: Promin, 1978.

Brzezinski, Zbigniew, ed., *Political Controls in the Soviet Army: A Study Based on Reports by Former Soviet Officers*. Research Program on the U.S.S.R., 1954.

Campbell, Ian, and Donald Macintyre, *The Kola Run*. London: Frederick Muller, 1958.

Cassidy, Henry C., *Moscow Dateline*. Houghton Mifflin, 1943.

Chuikov, Vasili I., *The Battle for Stalingrad*. Holt, Rinehart and Winston, 1964.

Clark, Alan, *Barbarossa: The Russian-German Conflict, 1941-45*. William Morrow, 1965.

Collins, James L., Jr., ed., *The Marshall Cavendish Illustrated Encyclopedia of World War II*. Marshall Cavendish, 1972.

Cooke, David C., and Martin Caidin, *Jets, Rockets and Guided Missiles*. McBride Company, 1951.

Culver, Bruce, *Panzer Colors II*. Squadron/Signal Publications, 1978.

Dallin, Alexander, *German Rule in Russia 1941-1945*. London: Macmillan, 1957.

Dyabinin, Boris, *Zapiski nachalnika tsekha*. Moscow: VTsSPS Profizdat, 1943.

"Effects of Climate on Combat in European Russia," U.S. Department of the Army, 1952.

Erickson, John:
Road to Stalingrad, The, Vol. 1. Harper & Row, 1975.
Soviet High Command, The. St. Martin's Press, 1962.

Flower, Desmond, *The Taste of Courage; The War, 1939-45*. Harper & Row, 1960.

Funcken, Liliane and Fred, *The Second World War*, Part 4. London: Ward Lock, 1976.

Gitlerovtsy nesut nam gore, muchenia i smert. Moscow: OGIZ, 1942.

Goerlitz, Walter, *Paulus and Stalingrad*. Citadel Press, 1963.

Great Patriotic War of the Soviet Union, 1941-1945. Moscow: Progress Publishers, 1970.

Green, William, *Famous Fighters of the Second World War*. Doubleday, 1975.

Green, William, and Gordon Swanborough, *Soviet Air Force Fighters*, Part 2. Arco Publishing, 1978.

Grove, Eric, *Russian Armour 1941-1943*. London: Almark Publishing, 1976.

Guillaume, Augustin, *Soviet Arms and Soviet Power*. Infantry Journal Press, 1949.

Halle, Armin, *Tanks: An Illustrated History of Fighting Vehicles*. New York Graphic Society, 1971.

Haupt, Werner, *Krim, Stalingrad, Kaukasus*. Friedberg: Podzun-Pallas-Verlag, 1977.

Hindus, Maurice, *Mother Russia*. Doubleday, Doran, 1943.

Hogg, Ian V.:
Encyclopedia of Infantry Weapons of World War II, The. Thomas Y. Crowell, 1977.
Guns: 1939-45, The. Ballantine Books, 1979.

Hogg, Ian V., and John Weeks, *Military Small Arms of the 20th Century*. Hippocrene Books, 1977.

Icks, Robert J., *Tanks and Armored Vehicles, 1900-1945*. Ed. by Phillip Andrews. WE Inc., no date.

Irving, David:
Destruction of Convoy PQ. 17, The. Simon and Schuster, 1968.
Hitler's War. Viking Press, 1977.

Istoria vtoroi mirovoi voiny 1939-1945. Moscow: Voyennoye izdatelstvo ministerstva oborony SSSR, Vol. 5, 1975; Vol. 6, 1976.

Jukes, Geoffrey, *Stalingrad, the Turning Point*. Ballantine Books, 1968.

Kerr, Walter, *The Russian Army: Its Men, Its Leaders and Its Battles*. London: Victor Gollancz, 1944.

Khrushchev, Nikita, *Khrushchev Remembers*. Ed. and transl. by Strobe Talbott. Little, Brown, 1970.

Kirk, John, and Robert Young Jr., *Great Weapons of World War II*. Bonanza Books, 1961.

Kolyshkin, I., *Submarines in Arctic Waters (Memoirs)*. Transl. by David Skvirsky. Moscow: Progress Publishers, 1966.

Korolkevich, A., *A muzy ne molchali . . .* Leningrad: Lenizdat, 1965.

Kreipe, Werner, et al., *The Fatal Decisions*. London: Michael Joseph, 1956.

Lauterbach, Richard E., *These Are the Russians*. Harper & Brothers, 1945.

Liddell, Hart, B. H.:
German Generals Talk, The. William Morrow, 1948.
History of the Second World War. G. P. Putnam's, 1970.

Mackintosh, Malcolm, *Juggernaut*. Macmillan, 1967.

Macksey, Kenneth, ed., *Tank: Facts and Feats*. Two Continents Publishing Group, 1973.

Macksey, Kenneth, and John H. Batchelor, *Tank: A History of the Armoured Fighting Vehicle*. Charles Scribner's, 1970.

Magid, A., *Soldaty v rabochikh vatnikakh*. Moscow: Znaniye, 1969.

Majdalany, Fred, *The Fall of Fortress Europe*. London: Hodder and Stoughton, 1968.

Manstein, Erich von, *Lost Victories*. London: Methuen, 1955.

Mikhailov, N., *Meeting the Challenge*. Moscow: Progress Publishers, 1970.

Milsom, John, *Russian Tanks 1900-1970*. Galahad Books, 1970.

Minz, I., *The Red Army*. International Publishers, 1943.

Mitchell, Donald W., *A History of Russian and Soviet Sea Power*. Macmillan, 1974.

Morison, Samuel Eliot, *History of United States Naval Operations in World War II*:
Vol. 1, *The Battle of the Atlantic, September 1939—May 1943*. Little, Brown, 1947.
Vol. 9, *The Atlantic Battle Won, May 1943—May 1945*. Little, Brown, 1968.

O'Ballance, Edgar, *The Red Army: A Short History*. Praeger, 1964.

Orgill, Douglas, *T-34 Russian Armor*. Ballantine Books, 1971.

Payne, Robert, *The Rise and Fall of Stalin*. Simon and Schuster, 1965.

"Peculiarities of Russian Warfare," U.S. Department of the Army, Historical Division, 1949.

Petrov, Evgeny, *Frontovoi dnevnik*. Moscow: Sovetsky pisatel, 1942.

Poliakov, Alexander, *White Mammoths*. E. P. Dutton, 1943.

Salisbury, Harrison E., *The Unknown War*. Bantam Books, 1978.

Schofield, Brian B., *The Russian Convoys*. Dufour Editions, 1964.

Schröter, Heinz, *Stalingrad*. E. P. Dutton, 1958.

Seaton, Albert:
Crimean War: A Russian Chronicle, The. St. Martin's Press, 1977.
Russo-German War 1941-45, The. Praeger, 1971.

Seth, Ronald, *Stalingrad: Point of Return*. Coward-McCann, 1959.

Sevastopol, November, 1941—July, 1942: Articles, Stories and Eye-Witness Accounts by Soviet War-Correspondents. London: Hutchinson & Co., 1943.

Simonov, Konstantin:
Days and Nights: Simon and Schuster, 1945.
Moscow. Moscow: Foreign Languages Publishing House, 1943.
Shtrikhi epopei. Tashkent: Gosudarstvennoye izdatelstvo khudozhestvennoi literatury UzSSR, 1961.

Smith, Hedrick, *The Russians*. Quadrangle (The New York Times Book Co.), 1976.

Stalingrad: An Eye-Witness Account by Soviet Correspondents and Red Army Commanders. London: Hutchinson & Co., 1959.

Storia Illustrata. December 1967.

Strategy & Tactics magazine, *War in the East: The Russo-German Conflict 1941-45*. Simulations Publications, 1977.

Svoim oruzhiyem. Moscow. Gosudarstvennoye izdatelstvo politicheskoi literatury, 1961.

Tarasov, K. K., and P. F. Khapunov, *Vozrozhdeniye*. Dnepropetrovsk: Promin, 1977.

Two Hundred Days of Fire: Accounts by Participants and Witnesses of the Battle of Stalingrad. Moscow: Progress Publishers, 1970.

Velikaya otechestvennaya voina 1941-1945. Planeta, 1941 vol., 1975; 1942 vol., 1976; 1943 vol., 1978.

Virski, Fred, *My Life in the Red Army*. Macmillan, 1949.

Vodolagin, M. A., *U sten Stalingrada*. Moscow: Gosudarstvennoye izdatelstvo politicheskoi literatury, 1958.

Voyetekhov, Boris, *The Last Days of Sevastopol*. Transl. by Ralph Parker and V. M. Genne. Knopf, 1943.

Voznesensky, Nikolai A., *The Economy of the USSR during World War II*. Public Affairs Press, 1948.

Weal, Elke C., *Combat Aircraft of World War Two*. Macmillan, 1977.

Werth, Alexander:
Russia At War, 1941-1945. E. P. Dutton, 1964.
Year of Stalingrad, The. London: Hamish Hamilton, 1946.

White, W. L., *Report on the Russians*. Harcourt, Brace, 1945.

Wilmot, Chester, *The Struggle for Europe*. Harper & Row, 1963.

Young, Peter, *Atlas of the Second World War*. Berkley Publishing, 1974.

Zhukov, Georgi K., *The Memoirs of Marshal Zhukov*. Delacorte Press, 1971.

Ziemke, Earl F., *Stalingrad to Berlin: The German Defeat in the East*. Office of the Chief of Military History, United States Army, 1968.

ACKNOWLEDGMENTS

For help given in the preparation of this book, the editors wish to express their gratitude to Sadie Alford, Novosti Press Agency, London; Hans Becker, ADN-Zentralbild, Berlin; Dana Bell, U.S. Air Force Still Photo Depository, 1361st Audio-Visual Squadron, Arlington, Virginia; Leroy Bellamy, Prints and Photographs Division, Library of Congress, Washington, D.C.; LaVerle Berry, Arlington, Virginia; Eva Bong, Ullstein Bilderdienst, Berlin; Carole Boutté, Senior Researcher, U.S. Army Audio-Visual Activity, Pentagon, Arlington, Virginia; Samuel Daniel, Prints and Photographs Division, Library of Congress, Washington, D.C.; V. M. Destefano, Chief of Reference Branch, U.S. Army Audio-Visual Activity, Pentagon, Arlington, Virginia; Victoria Edwards, Sovfoto, New York, New York; Tony Gale, Pictorial Press, London; Mary Lou Gjernes, U.S. Army Center for Military History, Alexandria, Virginia; Arthur Grimm, Berlin; Ilse Handt, Hamburg; Al Hardin, U.S. Army Library, Pentagon, Arlington, Virginia; Dr. Matthias Haupt, Bundesarchiv, Koblenz, Germany; Werner Haupt, Bibliothek für Zeitgeschichte, Stuttgart; E. C. Hine, Imperial War Museum, London; Heinrich Hoffmann, Hamburg; Jerry Kearns, Prints and Photographs Division, Library of Congress, Washington, D.C.; Heidi Klein, Bildarchiv Preussischer Kulturbesitz, Berlin; Dr. Roland Klemig, Bildarchiv Preussischer Kulturbesitz, Berlin; Gene Kubal, U.S. Army Library, Pentagon, Arlington, Virginia; Otto Kumm, Offenburg, Germany; William H. Leary, National Archives and Records Service, Audio-Visual Division, Washington, D.C.;

J. Lucas, Imperial War Museum, London; Mary Ann McNaughton, U.S. Army Center for Military History, Alexandria, Virginia; Rüdiger von Manstein, Irschenhausen, Germany; Brün Meyer, Bundesarchiv Militärarchiv, Freiburg, Germany; Meinhard Nilges, Bundesarchiv, Koblenz, Germany; Daniel E. O'Brien, Curator, Army Ordnance Museum, Aberdeen Proving Grounds, Aberdeen, Maryland; Thomas Oglesby, National Archives and Records Service, Audio-Visual Division, Washington, D.C.; Vladimir Perscin, Novosti Press Agency, Rome; Janusz Piekalkiewicz, Rösrath-Hoffnungsthal, Germany; Dr. Paul Schmidt-Carell, Hamburg; Jost W. Schneider, Wuppertal, Germany; Axel Schulz, Ullstein Bilderdienst, Berlin; Arlene Farber Sirkon, Chief, Still Photo Library Division, U.S. Army Audio-Visual Activity, Pentagon, Arlington, Virginia; James H. Trimble, Archivist, National Archives, Still Photo Branch, Washington, D.C.; Natalia Vikhliaev, Photolibrarian, Bureau Soviétique d'Information, Paris; Paul White, National Archives and Records Service, Audio-Visual Division, Washington, D.C.; A. Williams, Imperial War Museum, London; M. Willis, Imperial War Museum, London; Marjorie Willis, Radio Times Hulton Picture Library, London; Michael Winey, Curator of Special Collections, U.S. Army Military History Institute, Carlisle Barracks, Pennsylvania; Marie Yates, U.S. Army Audio-Visual Activity, Pentagon, Arlington, Virginia.

The index for this book was prepared by Nicholas J. Anthony.

INDEX

Numerals in italics indicate an illustration of the subject mentioned.

Printed in U.S.A.